8

TITANIA'S
NUMBER

8

Titania Hardie

CONNECTIONS
BOOK PUBLISHING

For my many friends who were born – like me – on the 17th!

A CONNECTIONS EDITION
This edition published in Great Britain in 2007 by
Connections Book Publishing Limited
St Chad's House, 148 King's Cross Road, London WC1X 9DH
www.connections-publishing.com

British Library Cataloguing-in-Publication data available on request.

ISBN 978-1-85906-230-2

1   3   5   7   9   10   8   6   4   2

Phototypeset in Bliss and Natural Script using QuarkXPress on Apple Macintosh
Printed in China

Contents

STARTING THE JOURNEY

This little book of numerology invites you to be amazed by what you will learn from numbers – about your character, your tastes, your instincts, your relationships, and even about your future. But to do this involves a willingness to believe – as Pythagoras, the 'Father of Numbers' did – that numbers can provide a clue, or formula, through which we can perceive some of the evolving patterns and cycles that affect our own individual existence.

Let's find out more ...

Discovering numerology

Fans of Sudoku will understand how it entices us intellectually to see how strands of numbers – almost magically – slot together and interconnect with one another, revealing a rhythm of harmonious relationships between the lines. In one sense, numerology does this for us on a personal and spiritual level. The Science of Numbers, as it is called, suggests that there is an order and a rhythm in the universe of which we are a part, and although there is a certain mystery in the way numbers seem to function as symbols for our experiences, there is a long tradition across many cultures of their fascination for us.

Now, in an age of gigabytes, PINs and mathematic-based technology, how can we doubt the role that numbers play, or the way in which they have become part of our daily landscape? Numbers speak to us every day about our personal identity on this planet. Our birth date is absorbed by society as proof of our existence: you need it to be 'real' at the bank, in the office, when you travel, in an automated phone queue – in *all* official records. Indeed, many people consider the day-date of their birthday to be their lucky number. But can it really say anything about us?

Did you know, for instance, that:

- If you were a **5** or a **9**, you'd need to invest in good-quality luggage because you'd be bound to notch up a lot of air miles?
- Or that a **4** will painstakingly spend hours getting something just right, whereas a **1** will rush in and get several projects started, full of enthusiasm, only to leave someone else to carry them through to completion?
- And a **3** is a born entertainer, who enjoys spending time with others, whereas a **2** prefers to live quietly,

with just one or two partnerships, both socially and in business?

But you've picked *this* little volume because you're an **8** – the most generous and, occasionally, spendthrift soul who will take everyone out to lunch on their bill! A **7**, on the other hand, is choosier about company, and guards their finances and privacy more, while a **6** prefers to cook at home for their extended family.

About this book

Each individual title in this series investigates, in depth, the meaning of one of nine personal numbers. *This* volume is dedicated to the exploration of the number **8**.

We will be focusing principally on your **DAY** number – that is, the number relating to the day of the month on which you were born (in your case, the 8th, 17th or 26th of the month) Calculating your **DAY** number is easy: you simply add the digits of your day together (where applicable), and keep adding them until they reduce to a single number (*see calculation examples on page 270*). And that's it. It doesn't matter which month or year you were born in – you just need the day-date to discover your **DAY** number. And *you're* an **8.**

Your **DAY** number reveals all kinds of information, and, working from this number, we will be considering:

- The obvious attributes of your number as they impact on your personality
- How you are likely to dress, and what colours or styles appeal
- How you react to things psychologically, and what drives or motivates you
- In which fields you will have the most natural abilities and gifts

| 8 | 9 | 1 | 2 | 3 | 4 | 5 | 6 | 7 |

- What annoys you most
- What sort of lover you are, and how you relate to all other numbers
- What the future holds

... and much, much more.

And you have another significant number too: your **LIFE** number. This is derived from adding up the digits in the *whole* of your birth date – day, month and year (*see examples on page 270*). What does *this* number mean, and what do your **DAY** and **LIFE** numbers mean in tandem? And how does it affect you if you're also a 'master' number (**11** or **22**)? Read on and you'll see. But first, let's meet your **DAY** number ...

7   6   5   4   3   2   1   9   8

So, you're an 8

Forceful, with a huge **determination**, you came to this world with an inherent sense of experience and judgement. Your nature is to make things happen, to feel the extraordinary possibility that is life, to **push the boundaries**. You can harness your exceptionally clear and **dynamic mind** to any task and make a difference, which is why **8** rises to the top in business and is usually self-employed, or head of a larger force. Your number says **'wisdom'** learned from **inherited experience: 8**s bring divine awareness and karmic truth with them to the cradle. Fair-minded and **intellectually rigorous**, you ponder the mysteries of the human soul and of the earth.

Every number is predominantly feminine or masculine, but in the number **8** – symbolized by two circles of infinity

8	9	1	2	3	4	5	6	7

– both male and female awareness reside. This gives you the strength and **willpower** that is traditionally male, but the grace and **fair judgement** that is associated with the female. You understand all that is given within the heavens and the earth – the conflicts of rich and poor, of ill and well, of action and inaction, of kindness and discipline. Your number represents **authority without prejudice**, and this ideal you will strive for throughout your lifetime.

Let us say what is outstanding about this number. When your mind is focused on positivity and **selflessness**, you have the opportunity to bring **hope** and energy where it is lacking. With an enormous capacity for **self-discipline** and effort, you can alter the outcome of a difficult situation and actually change the material world around you. Not always aware of the way the great **power** within you may work, you nevertheless understand that the human race has only scratched the surface of what may be attained.

Until there is **balance** between effort and rest, between

7 6 5 4 3 2 1 9 8

differing viewpoints of culture and faith, between masculine and feminine principles, between give and take, we are
only in our infancy. **8** wishes to build **celestial possibilities**
on earth. Nothing less than this is **8**'s mission and inner
drive. It is an exhausting demand but a personal priority,
and astonishing **mental powers** and good judgement come
to your aid. You are undeniably at your best when both
efficient in your energies and impartial in your analysis.

And now let us look at the challenge of this number.
For an **8**, the most important personal striving is towards
balance. The two circles of the number represent the scales
of moral integrity and spirituality alongside material need
and physical effort. With an intense feeling about what is
right, **8**s become **angry at injustice** – and even emotional
and **impatient**, if bureaucracy or blindness obstructs the
process of natural and moral law. If **personal ambition**
becomes the be-all and end-all, money may become a
problem instead of a tool at your disposal. When you bal-

ance the moral, spiritual and emotional factors of life with the material and the physical, extraordinary opportunities are given to you. No number can find greater **success** and influence – provided you **direct your gifts** with a philosophical and **impartial** mind.

Many times over, life will demand that you repeat your efforts to get something right. **8**s want to give one-hundred-and-ten per cent to everything, and are hurt and angered when others don't operate the same way. Long periods of **sustained effort** are required, which can be frustrating and tiring; but no one has more courage or **resilience**. Patience will come, and once you've found the formula towards work and effort, **kindness** and **tenacity**, the dream can be made real. This is part of **8**'s profile.

For the best chance of happiness and success, use your **shrewd** mind and **resourceful** spirit to exert some control on the circumstances around you. **8**s have everything it takes to be a financial success, and if you fail at one thing you'll redouble your efforts. **8**s don't give up without a fight: you have the power to be a serious moneymaker, yet to be **generous** and philanthropic with it. Perhaps you could be best understood as a **realistic idealist**. Only if you are truly thwarted or unloved will you lapse into domineering ruthlessness. **8**'s higher nature will try to offset such a plunge! Great **inspiration** and originality should lift you out of the mire when you start to sink at times.

Sound familiar? Getting a taste for what your number is about? And this is just the beginning. You'll soon find out how the number 8 expresses itself as your Day number in each and every day of your life. But before we go any further, let's take a look at where all this first came from ...

8   9   1   2   3   4   5   6   7

What's in a number?

Numbers have always had a sacred meaning. The Egyptians used an alphabet that conflated letters and numbers, and, as such, each number exuded an idea that was more than the sum it stood for. There is a whole book of the Old Testament devoted to the subject; and the Hebrew language – exactly like the Egyptian – has a magical subtext of meaning where letters and numbers can be doubled to reveal an extra layer of secret, so-called 'occult' information. It is called the *gematria*, and forms a crucial part of the sacred occult wisdom called Kabbalah. There were twenty-two letters – a master number – in both the Greek (Phoenician) and Hebrew alphabets, and repetitions of the spiritual properties of the numbers **3** and, especially, **7** recur throughout the Bible.

7   6   5   4   3   2   1   9   8

The Father of Numbers

But modern numerology derives more formally from Pythagoras, the Father of Numbers, who was a serious and spiritual philosopher, as well as the man who explained some of the secrets of geometry. Born on the island of Samos, although he ultimately settled in Cretona, a Greek colony in southern Italy, he is understood to have travelled widely to both Egypt and Judea. Some accounts of his life also suggest he may have studied under the Persian sages of Zoroaster, but an analysis of his teachings certainly reveals the strong influence of Kabbalistic thought in his philosophy.

Pythagoras understood numbers as a *quality* of being, as well as a *quantity* of material value. In one sense, the numbers as figures were connected with the measuring of things, but 'number' itself was significantly different to this, and encompassed a spiritual value. The numbers from one through to nine represented universal principles through which everything evolves, symbolizing even the stages an idea passes through before it becomes a reality. Mathematics was the tool through which we could apprehend the Creation, the universe, and ourselves. Musical harmony was a sacred part of this knowledge, as was geometry, which revealed divine proportion.

Most importantly, Pythagoras believed that numbers were expressive of the principles of all real existence – that numbers themselves embodied the principles of our dawning awareness, our conjecture and growth. Through mathematics and number we could approach divine wisdom and the workings of the universe as a macrocosm. Thus, in microcosm, our personal 'mathematics' would unlock the workings of our own being, and help us to see a divine wisdom concerning ourselves. **1** was not just the first digit, but also had a character of beginning, of independence, of leadership, just as the number **2** was more than merely the second number quantifying two objects, but also implied the philosophical concept of a pair, of co-operation, of a relationship beyond the individual.

Pythagoras also believed that we could understand our direction and fate through an awareness of repeating cycles of number, making numerology a key to revealing our opportunities and our destiny.

By tradition, the doctrine Pythagoras taught to his students in the sixth century BCE was secret, and no one wrote down his ideas until his death. But Plato was a follower of Pythagoras and, along with the rebirth of Platonism, the ideas of the Father of Mathematics were revealed afresh during the revival of Greek learning in the Renaissance. The great magi of the fifteenth and sixteenth centuries explored anew the significance of number and the gematria, to understand the hidden messages of the ancients and of the divine mind. Mathematics as a philosophy was the bridge to higher realms of spirituality.

Essence of the numbers

one is the spark, the beginning, Alpha, the Ego of consciousness. It is male.

two is consort. Adding partnership, receptivity, it is female, bringing tact.

three is a synthesizing of both of these qualities and brings expansion and joy.

four is the number of the Earth, of the garden, and of stability. It brings order.

five is curiosity and experiment, freedom, changes. It brings sensuality.

six nurtures and cares for others. It will love and beautify, and brings counsel.

seven perfects and contemplates the Creation. It is intellect, stillness, spirit.

eight is the number of power, the octave, a higher incarnation. It brings judgement.

nine is humanity, selflessness, often impersonal and all-knowing. It brings compassion.

7 6 5 4 3 2 1 9 8

Applying the knowledge

A deeper understanding of the self can be achieved through an awareness of the mysticism of number within us; and both the birth date and, to some degree, our given name are the keys to unlocking our mystical, spiritual core of being. Exploring the affinity between letter and number can also reveal insights about the lessons we need to learn throughout our lives to improve and develop as individuals (*see page 25*).

This book looks at the significance of numbers as they affect us every day, focusing largely, as introduced earlier, on our DAY number. It is this number that reveals to us our instincts, our impulses, our natural tastes and undiluted responses, our talents and immediate inclinations. This is how people see us in daily situations, and how we behave by essence.

We will be exploring how our DAY number influences

8   9   1   2   3   4   5   6   7

our love relationships and friendships; at what it says about our career strengths and our childhood; at the way our number manifests in our leisure time; and at how it might give us a better understanding of what to expect in our future cycles, as we pass through any given year under the sway of a particular number. Each birthday initiates a new cycle, and each cycle seems uncannily connected with the philosophical concerns of the number which governs that year. Look both to the past and present to see how strongly the number-cycle can illuminate our experiences ... and then count ahead to ponder what may be in store over the next year or two.

And numbers also say something about where we live or work, about our car, and even about our pets. Understanding these secret qualities can add a new dimension of pleasure – not to mention surprise – to our journey through life.

7   6   5   4   3   2   1   9   8

A NUMBER TO GROW INTO

The presence of our **LIFE** number, however, takes longer for us to appreciate in ourselves – longer for us to grow into; and it often takes time to reveal itself. This number comes to the fore as your life progresses, and on pages 214–247 we will be looking at the meaning of your **DAY** number together with your individual **LIFE** number, to see what this reveals about your character and potentiality.

The **LIFE** number may intensify the experience of the **DAY** number – if it is closely related to it, or shares similar patterns. But more frequently our two different numbers clash a little, and this often allows insight into the aspects of our being where instinct pulls us in one direction but higher wisdom or experience mediates and pulls us in a second direction.

Who would have thought you could learn so much from a number? Pythagoras certainly did, over 2,500 years ago ... and now you will discover it too.

What's in a name?

Your name also has a story to tell, and it is a story revealed through number. Every letter corresponds to a number: in the Western alphabet we use twenty-six letters, which are at variance with the twenty-two formerly enshrined in the Hebrew and Greek alphabets. Some numerologists believe that this is in keeping with the more material world we now live in, as the number '26' reduces to '8' (when you add the digits), which is the number of power and money.

The correspondences between the numbers and the letters of the alphabet are as follows:

1	2	3	4	5	6	7	8	9
A	B	C	D	E	F	G	H	I
J	K	L	M	N	O	P	Q	R
S	T	U	V	W	X	Y	Z	

7	6	5	4	3	2	1	9	8

As you are an **8**, it is most revealing to look at the letters H, Q and Z, as they occur (or not!) in your name. This is because they intensify the experience and impression of your main number.

To make the most of the qualities inherent in your number, you should be using a name which is in poetic harmony with your **DAY** number. As an **8**, you feel the need to achieve and to *do*, and you will be at your most successful and efficient every day if you have a name which underlines these strong **8** qualities. Using a name which includes an H, Q or Z bolsters your powers. If this sounds strange, consider that many of us have our names shortened or played upon by friends, family and lovers, so it is important to feel that our chosen name – the one that we use as we go about in the world – is making the best of our abilities and energies.

Among the letters that are equivalent to the number **8**, H is a relatively common consonant – so the chances are you have this letter in your name, especially partnered with a 't' or an 's' as a digraph. It is particularly significant if your name starts with one of these, or if the first letter is an '8' letter, because this strengthens the power of your number **8** at the beginning of your name. Create a nickname with it in, if necessary, to back up the outstanding properties of dynamism that come with your number.

The letter-numbers help us to act out our sense of purpose, and if these work in correspondence with the DAY number we are more likely to find our sense of will and achieve our goals more rapidly. But if we have few, or none, of the letters of our DAY number, we often feel it is much harder to shine in our field of opportunity.

Missing an '8' letter?

As an **8**, you rely on demonstrating your feelings to others, but if you have no '**8**' letters in your name you may be

7   6   5   4   3   2   1   9   8

finding it hard to earn or hold on to money, or to express balance in relationships; you might also be unable to organize work and your domestic life comfortably.

8 rules business so completely that a lack of this letter-number through your name (or nickname) can often cause you to feel frustration in your career – or, even, doubt that you will ever be entirely comfortable with your work life. Find a way to work an '**8**' letter into your life – as a company or a pet name, for instance, or by playing with the spelling of your name. Then you will gain confidence about the way the world sees and responds to you.

Too many 'H's or 'Z's?

It can be just as much of a problem if your name carries a flood of letters which correspond to your number. Just as a lack of 'H's could make you a little ungenerous or less free-flowing in your instincts, a surfeit could make you

| 8 | 9 | 1 | 2 | 3 | 4 | 5 | 6 | 7 |

spendthrift or overly power-hungry! More than three will add an extra dose of ambition, but you may be either very wealthy or very poor: balance is harder to achieve with too many '**8**' letters!

Many 'H's can also make you a nature-lover, but inclined to nervous strain. Several 'Q's, on the other hand, give you a strongly mystical side, while Z is considered the major achiever. With all three in your name, be careful not to dictate to others, or to attempt to control everyone you love.

YOUR DAY NUMBER
It's a new day ...

You will learn a lot about the numbers of your birthday and your name as this book unfolds, but the DAY number is, to my mind, the most important – and sometimes least well-recognized – number of all ... the number which exerts a magnetic hold on us each and every day of our lives. Every time we react to a situation, an emotion, a provocation of any kind, we are shooting straight from the hip, as it were, and this reaction is coloured by our DAY number.

8 9 1 2 3 4 5 6 7

As we know, your 'Day Force', or **DAY**, number is **8** if you were born on the 8th, 17th or 26th of any month. Each of these different dates also affects us – the characteristics of the number derived from a birthday on the 8th vary intriguingly from one on the 26th, for instance – and we will look at these differences in the pages ahead.

All three dates, however, still reconcile to an overall **8**. This number determines your gut reactions and the way you express yourself when you are being most true to yourself. Your parents, lovers, friends and co-workers all know you best through this number.

So what is the theme of being an 8? What are you like when you're at work, rest and play? And how compatible are you with the other numbers? Let's find out …

7 6 5 4 3 2 1 9 8

8'S CHARACTER
Charms, graces, warts and all ...

A number of great tasks and burdens, of sheer force of will and determination to succeed, 8 is a mystery. Truly so. Desperate to see the logical and sensible truths about our existence and yet drawn inexorably to higher, spiritual ponderings, 8 is the sceptic and the occultist rolled into one. This number refers to God – however you may see that – and also to the 'music of the spheres'. The octave is dependent on this number, and there is an underlying push for all 8s to grapple with the idea of *harmony*, in all its possible meanings.

8 9 1 2 3 4 5 6 7

Power to the people

In the number spectrum from **1** to **9**, **5** is the halfway point, marking the place where life on planet earth – the actual, physical planet – departs from life in the cerebrum, and in the upper world of the spirit. **6** is the number of conscientious feeling for others, **7** of seeking truths and answers, and **8** the number that assumes power. It is the number of karma, absorbing an inherent knowledge of all that has been before somewhere in its inner being.

As an **8**, then, you will understand at the deepest level that you will reap exactly what you have sown, and that power comes to you in relation to the time you have spent training your intellect and your physical and emotional energies in the understanding of a successful, harmonious existence. To find a balance between earth and sky, individual and universal, god and man – to uncover whatever is divine in the human form – is the will and the creed of **8**.

7   6   5   4   3   2   1   9   8

The strength within

From your childhood, others have expected a great deal from you. Blessed with a fierce determination to succeed at whatever it is that interests you – and this may be everything from sports to music, and from academic prowess to a role in front of the public – you have great reserves of strength and a memory your friends will envy, which will propel you forward. You always tackle the most difficult jobs, the most demanding goals, so that you can rise above the banal; and you are entirely likely to succeed in such endeavours, and come to the pinnacle of success. Time and again, you will rely on your own inner strengths to overcome obstacles and adversity; and, time and again, you are the crutch for others to lean on.

The wider world recognizes your innate authority and admires your dynamic personality. You may appear as a quietly dignified and reliable centred human being, or as a more vibrant and forceful character; either way, you exude that executive status that makes others trust and look up to you. Sometimes this is simply because you look affluent and confident, but it is also because you have the look of the judge, rather than the cleric, about you. You are ethical and unbiased, and you have learned from a lifetime of personal experience that it is important to have all the facts. This often means you acquire a great personal library en route to higher knowledge – and we're talking here of reference books and beautifully crafted hard-cover volumes, which will adorn your shelves and furnish your mind.

Infinite wisdom

As your number is uniquely both masculine and feminine – based on its shape of infinity and the two interlocking circles – you are capable of being directed and instructed, but also of being the strong guide of others. Masculine and feminine energies represent all that exists in the celestial and physical worlds, and bringing them into harmony allows for the extraordinary realization of some semi-divine achievements. It is also vital that these energies co-exist within you, for separating them causes strife and discord.

This partly explains the inner conflicts you may feel – between what is right for you personally and what is in the interests of others in the wider community. The pendulum of your nature swings widely in opposite directions, and will confuse those who know you. You are so often extravagantly – recklessly – generous, and yet at times you are strikingly measured in your gestures of goodwill. This surprises you as much as anyone.

Emotionally, you may be exceptionally patient, giving and selfless, yet also excessively demanding and repressive of others' feelings. These inconsistencies will frustrate you, but it is easier to understand when you know that it is towards *balance*, the fruitful harnessing of the pendulum's

Keynotes of the 8 personality

Positive associations: astonishing stamina, broad understanding of personal/emotional/global issues, control, responsibility, musical, sporty, courageous, motivated, charismatic, possessed of great will

Negative associations: tension, stressed by things moving too slowly, too forceful, impatient, occasionally greedy, over-emphasis on material life, ambitious in an unbalanced way, demanding of recognition

swinging energy, that you are striving. Once **8** comprehends – almost instinctively – the whole picture, it moves into a higher realm of knowledge. But this is a tall order, too. Balance demands the effort expended to understand *both* sides of all debate; the need for both material security and spiritual enlightenment; for responsibility to others and the desire to fulfil personal ambitions. It may take time!

| 7 | 6 | 5 | 4 | 3 | 2 | 1 | 9 | 8 |

Sartorial sense

Your personal style is one of either distinction or dynamism, but never flamboyance. You recognize very clearly the importance of looking successful – partly to inspire confidence in others. For you, clothes should be well-tailored and made of the finest materials, and you understand the sense of investment-buying.

With an eye for quality, you will choose – by preference – expensive items that are classically designed, which will become staples for years. You are unlikely to be comfortable in cheap clothes, but sometimes this becomes an obsession and you will spend beyond your budget to have the wardrobe you feel you need to make an impact. **8**s may also over-gild the lily at times, wearing too much jewellery or too many accessories – but they will not be cheap imitations, if you can help it! 'Thrift' is never an **8**'s favourite word.

| 8 | 9 | 1 | 2 | 3 | 4 | 5 | 6 | 7 |

Lessons for life

In your clever and retentive mind, you love to intellectualize and work out the psychological motives behind every significant action and decision. Your excellent judgement and mental powers are part of what brings money into your life, but aside from this, you are fascinated by philosophy and the way to approach a happy or meaningful existence. You have a knack for understanding the relationship between feelings and incidents, almost as though the intuitive, feminine side of your otherwise masculine intellect sees the emotional response to external stimuli. Thus, you know very quickly why someone acts or speaks as they do.

This makes you an even wiser counsellor than **7**, who possesses the analytical skills but not always the empathetic feeling (which is more common in a **2**). You, additionally, have the mental acuity to understand the remedial action necessary when things have gone awry – as long as

7 6 5 4 3 2 1 9 **8**

it is in relation to someone else! To see the difficulty in your own affairs is much harder, for either your masculine or feminine side will dominate at any given time. When you can rise above the personal, hurt reaction to a difficult event, you will usually act – as ever – without prejudice or illusion. Many hard-learned lessons have taught you how to do this. Never static, **8** learns and digests an understanding of human action throughout life.

Reach for the sky

Something within compels you to give your all to everything you do. The **8** student will work harder than their classmates to execute the most original and thoroughly produced project, just as the grown-up **8** executive will scour the land looking for the right people to contribute to original projects and new ideas. **8** doesn't want to replicate, but prefers to teach the world to sing new songs and dance to new rhythms. This translates to personal relationships: the **8** parent goes all out to create a birthday party for their child that others wouldn't even have been able to dream of; and, in a love bond, the partner of an **8** will be spoiled – not just materially, but inventively.

To put it simply, **8** thinks of things no one else does – not so much because of a vivid imagination or creativity as because, to an **8**, everything is possible. Nothing's out of bounds. Any serious goal brings out the best in you, and it is this quality that makes you a born leader. Brimming with inspirational ideas and talents, you can accomplish anything you think worthwhile. Persistence and diplomacy help you in this respect, and you will choose the partners in life who have something to contribute to your goals. Even in love, you must find a partner you can respect, and who excites your mind and originality. This sounds as though relationships are of convenience, but it's more that they must spark your enthusiasm and excite your willpower.

7   6   5   4   3   2   1   9   8

Music to your ears

And, speaking of creativity and inspiration, it is hard to imagine an **8** who is not transformed by music. With a genuine talent that may often go untrained, **8**s have an ear for sounds of all kinds – in the human voice as well as in music or melody – and also a strong feeling for rhythm. This will make you a good amateur dancer or instrumentalist, as well as an authoritative speaker. It is this sense of rhythm that often makes **8**s outstanding sportspeople, too.

Your strength is in the way you hear things – or, even, *what* you hear. You may listen carefully to rain and wind, and hear more than the weather. Memory based on hearing is very strong, and if something is spoken to you in a particular way, it may lodge for eternity. All harmonies transport you, and it can be a religious experience hearing complex, woven melodies or instrumentation. Sounds such as this lift your soul very high.

8	9	1	2	3	4	5	6	7

The sweet spell of success

We looked earlier at the importance of the letters in your name, and how the name you use can help you to attain your extraordinary destiny. The number **8** brings with it certain demands on your private time, and the frequent need to be selfless in everyday life. This is tough sometimes, when your feet ache and your mind is tired, and you want to curl up and recover your spirits. But using an '**8**' letter somewhere in your name or nickname will ennoble you, and help you fight off fatigue.

It is necessary to remember why you are doing something, and what you are fighting for. Understand that **8**'s duty is to make a reality of the earthly dream of divine creation and balance, and that there is a sense of divine command for the number **8** to answer to. This is not a branded command, or even a traditionally religious outlook; but **8** has spiritual duties, to be a noble and wise

7 6 5 4 3 2 1 9 **8**

judge – to be, effectively, the 'Solomon of numbers'. Using an **8** power-letter helps to lift you out of the banal and into the inspirational, but it also helps you to control your finances and use material reward to greater benefit.

Lead the way

An **8** child is already learning to landscape a terrain of dreams and plans for a different life from the very first years of creative intelligence. Every **8** performs best, and finds their best individual expression, when they have a serious goal or purpose to espouse. To make your life happy, in other words, you need to design an idea or end product that will be useful *and* beautiful, *and* of substance for the community.

Your strength here is to be able to lead, originate and oversee the actualization of a worthy project – even if that project is originally the dream of someone else. You are less likely to fall over success or fortuitous money as easily and naturally as a **6** or a **3**, but you are certain to achieve astonishing results – and even riches – as the prize from your own expended effort, and from your exceptional abilities. What comes to you is earned and merited, not stumbled across by luck. This is one reason why the proper training and disciplining of your mind and talents should be a priority; don't expect luck to simply descend upon you!

Get the balance right

If you find yourself perpetually troubled by money matters or business stresses that appear to come from the outside world, you may be placing a disproportionate emphasis on accruing wealth or renown. Life may ask you to start over, and you may feel your exceptional will threatened, and your energies or spirit broken. These baffling struggles are designed to make you dig deeper, into your moral self. Remember: you have the inherent order placed upon you to be the judge, and wisdom must be gained for such a role. Being a judge – in this truly spiritual sense – also demands that you are aware of the decree that, as ye judge, so shall ye be judged. Such metamorphic events bring you, in time, to excellent handling of your affairs and the ability to master problems smoothly. You are the rock in any desperate storm.

In personal relationships, and even in business liaisons, fight the wish to be everything to everyone. You need not master every skill, nor wear yourself out in the pursuit of the high purposes you set your mind towards. You are a doer rather than a talker, but finding the balance between effort and rest is almost a divine command. Life will be much happier when you gain patience and allow yourself to be truly loved. You are so extremely resourceful, and have such a philosophical turn of mind, that you will always find the power to surmount trying periods. In seven days the earth is said to have been created; **8**, then, is the gateway to paradise.

8 in a nutshell

Personality watchwords: charismatic, efficient, good-humoured, forceful will

Lucky colours: opal, ivory, bronze

Lucky herbs/flowers: sunflower/moon-flower, peony, orchid, belladonna, rue

Scents: peony, vanilla, gardenia, jasmine

Fashion style: expensively cut well-designed clothes, sensual fabrics

Decorative style: impression of light and space, good design, a little 'razzle-dazzle'

Letters: H, Q or Z (needed in the name you use)

Car style: *quality* – second-hand, if necessary

Holiday destination: summer resorts of cities of power – New York/Rome and the Seychelles

7   6   5   4   3   2   1   9   8

Which 8 are you?

4 5 6 7 **8** 9 1 2 3

Everyone with a **DAY** number of **8** will exhibit many of the characteristics just discussed. It is interesting to see, though, how the number **8** varies across all of its incarnations. There is a subtle but definite difference between the way the number operates for someone born on the 8th of the month – which makes for a pure **8** effect – and someone born, say, on the 26th.

As a rule, anyone born on the single-digit date has the truest and most undiluted effect from the number, whereas someone born as a product of two digits borrows some qualities from the pairing of the numbers. Twenty-anything puts the softening digit '2' before the second number, and this usually means that, whatever number you are, you are more aware of the needs of others. Similarly, if '1' is the first digit (17th) you are more independent, and perhaps more assured of your self-worth, than other **8** people.

Let's look at the variations across all the birthdays ...

Born on the 8th?

With the pure form of **8**, yours is a power birthday! Success, leadership, recognition and advancement can all be yours. You have a finely balanced sense of moral truth – because your number is the true '**8**' symbol – and you understand how the pendulum of life may swing one way in one moment, and back again the next. You are generally quite ready for such shifts.

Blessed with the 'money number' in its purest form, you have strong leadership qualities, and are more progressive than traditionalist. You have excellent creative talent – markedly in both literature and music – and you will succeed wherever you place yourself in the business world, if you can simply find the best outlet for your skills. Enjoying what you do is the most important criterion. You always manage to channel your energies to create changes

| 8 | 9 | 1 | 2 | 3 | 4 | 5 | 6 | 7 |

in stagnant situations, and you have an undeniable executive ability. Add to this the fact that you are a good judge of character and yearn to get on with things, and you can see the potential for real success in life.

Although **8** is not exactly a 'lucky' number – results coming from effort and brainpower more than good luck – it is true to say that the 8th is considered the luckiest '**8**' birthday. However, to make the best of it you will need to utilize all of the opportunities which come to you, otherwise financial troubles may still be a possibility. Be certain, though, that this can be avoided by living a positive life with strong self-discipline and a respect for those moral and philosophical understandings that balance the push towards financial achievement. Learn to recognize your luck, and realize that you do have the power to attract what you need when you *really* need it.

You enjoy making a vivid impression on the world around you, and often indulge in a little flamboyance, too.

7 6 5 4 3 2 1 9 8

You probably have a yearning for a big house and good-quality clothes, and for making an entertaining entrance and achieving a little humorous notoriety. You may also want to build a good reference library, especially if you can acquire beautifully produced tomes – but you may never get round to reading all that you collect! This is true of your music collection, too, and you prefer to own the best of whatever you can afford.

Your mind sifts ideas that interest you, and you have deep thoughts on varied subjects – everything from politics to religion and even sex! There are few no-go zones for any number **8**, least of all someone with your pure birthday. It's possible that you're also excited by serious occult subjects, and, like all the **8**s, you have a progressive and open-minded approach to many different religious viewpoints.

For career fulfilment you need a broad canvas upon which to express yourself. You would make an excellent lawyer or legal counsel, and if you can balance law with other material concerns, or even with medicine, you would flourish. The 8th gives you the abilities of the executive — the overseas buyer or marketer, the personnel head-hunter, or the role of company director. However, as **8**'s talents are so diverse, you would also thrive as a truly creative and high-profile accountant, a member of an orchestra — especially working in film or theatre — or in commercial banking and the stock exchange. Many highly successful athletes and musicians have this birthday.

You have an excellent ear, and you respond to the voices of all who come into contact with you; this is a finely tuned sense for you, and you base your decisions on whether to trust or believe someone partly on how they sound inside your soul. Just like number 17, listening intently often tells you if things are 'right'. Born on the 8th, you will need to accept responsibilities and handle them as well as possible.

7   6   5   4   3   2   1   9   8

Born on the 17th?

Corresponding to the tarot card known as 'The Star', the 17th is quite a fortunate birthday if you harness your exceptional gift for using your wish-power and focusing on a clear end result. However, you will be tested often throughout your life for your willingness to smile through the worst rainstorms. This you can do, for you are lit with an inner strength and can frequently lift your saddened spirit out of the doldrums of personal or business adversity to shine on through, like that proverbial star.

You are the best researcher and investigator of all the 8s, and you love delving into enticing, mind-teasing mysteries. Many friends and family members see you as a very deep and introspective soul who needs some quiet time for philosophical musings. High-minded and surprisingly conservative at times, you can be progressive, extravagant

8   9   1   2   3   4   5   6   7

and unconventionally inspirational at others. You are also honest, with a desire to reveal the truth, and you like others to be straightforward with you – yet you have a particular skill in looking well below the obvious, and pursuing hidden areas of knowledge. You may be quite tough in business or in your expectations of others, becoming maddened if those you rely on come to repeat blunders or demonstrate inefficiency. Outside the work arena, though, you have a kind and considerate nature.

Although your birthday is quite spiritual, and fuels an inclination to ask questions of the great unknown, you're not gullible, requiring some proof of conclusions offered by others about things beyond the physical senses. However, **8**, your base number, is the karmic number, so you understand the idea of cause and effect; this gives you an inherent understanding of mystical and philosophical matters, and perhaps you need no proof of some 'truths' besides your own well-adjudged sense of what may be probable.

7   6   5   4   3   2   1   9   8

You have a keen appreciation of music, and hear the music of the spheres within – and indeed, like pure **8**, your listening skills are discerning. You also have an excellent facility for bringing forth inspired ideas, like a pinprick of light in the darkest night sky. If powerful mental application is then required from you, this is something you relish. You endure gruelling times and may be submerged by tests of your goodwill, but you have excellent powers for redis-covering the wellspring of hope and faith in the future. Strangely, the spiritual love and compassion you have for others gives you very good health for most of your life.

A proud parent, you are caring of your family and gen-erous about their abilities and achievements. Unlikely to forget others' birthdays – or, indeed, what they like – you enjoy showering those you love with beautiful quality gifts and surprises, as do most **8**s. You can be swayed by your emotions but are usually clear in your expectations. Once you make up your mind, you rarely shift from your path.

Business will be most fruitful for you if you use your executive or leadership qualities, and you won't mind going out into mid-ocean on your own sometimes. Delegate routine or mundane work. Some people with this birthday enjoy working in banking and property, or, if you choose writing as a career, you should draw on your research and love-of-mystery skills. All **8**s have a profound interest in history, and what has been before in the realm of thought. An **8** must conjecture, must have a subject to contemplate, and this is truest of you because of the numbers **1** and **7** both influencing your birth date. Careers involving history/research, criticism, acting, theatre production, publishing, broking, or taking the directive for other people, all work for you. The Star flavouring the birthday number also suggests an interest in astrology, numerology and serious psychic research. Although you must build your own bridges in life, you may amass a secure inheritance for your own children.

7   6   5   4   3   2   1   9   8

Born on the 26th?

This birthday seems to bring financial success and general good luck. It is the most karmic of the **8** incarnations, suggesting you will learn – and have been learning – about life from your earliest memories (perhaps some of which predate the cradle?). Believe that trying situations and tensions will build your strength and self-confidence over time; what you gain in life will be from the efforts you have put in, and from the philosophical conclusions you have reached. Growing confidence and awareness eventually comes to mean personal prosperity and happiness.

You probably have an interest in art – courtesy of the **2** and **6** lending their energy to your number **8** – but you will possibly do better career-wise in a straight business arena. With your enthusiasm and courage you can be an excellent organizer on the grandest scale; you need the scope to develop this talent. Resist the occasional urge to laziness, which sometimes comes from easy-going **6**, and don't give in to bouts of negativity, and you should never go short financially. Like all **8**s, your monetary fortune rests with *you*. Experience will bring a balanced appreciation of the importance material freedom can offer you – along with a feeling of responsibility to the world around you. **6**'s kind heart and **2**'s desire be of service to others combine to give you an altruistic concern for other people.

Being quite impulsive, you may start several projects and ventures but leave them for others to finish. Try to concentrate your efforts. This is even true in your personal life, where that rashness that might at best be called 'spontaneity' leads you into sudden, intense love relationships, until personal hurt and the wisdom you gain offer you another perspective. Your sudden moves and emotions can cause confusion for the people around you, and this gets you into hot water at times. Don't, however, go on

with self-recrimination for past folly for years and years:
all **8**s have a tendency to live a little too much in the past,
and this may be especially true of you. Try to move on, to
be optimistic and look to the future with enthusiasm.

Do you love ceremony and grand occasions? You can
be a generous host and great party-thrower, and public
demonstrations of landmarks and personal milestones are
usually worth the effort. You will blossom if given a wide
education from good study, books, travel, and in the whole
of life; travel or living abroad may especially suit you. You
are a philosopher, and have a proud mind and strong sense
of purpose. Home and children are a happy demand on
your time and emotions. You also experience moody cycles,
when your feelings soar and plummet at intervals. A strong
emotional relationship will help you to level this out – but
even your partner may scratch their head at times!

Once you achieve a predominant state of self-control
and pragmatism, you should rise to a position of power and

8   9   1   2   3   4   5   6   7

considerable influence in your career — but find someone to delegate the menial tasks to! **8** is a mental worker and never a labourer. Law, publishing, education, accounting, music and corporate work are good areas for your talents to shine in. You are also a very gifted public speaker, which may lead you into lecturing or other public roles, even including government positions and ambassadorial jobs. You definitely need to work for yourself, or in partnership, being a boss rather than an employee.

As mentioned earlier, **8**s have excellent rhythm and often excel in music. Whether you sing or play, music will be the audio-wallpaper of your world. You also have that number **8** occult inclination — which is all about digging into nature's secrets, and questing after the hidden meanings of life. You may also be quite religious, and yours is the number of considerable sensuality. **8** is related to the star sign Scorpio, with similar interests in life and death, love and money, secrets, and deep thought.

7   6   5   4   3   2   1   9   8

8 AT WORK

So, what kind of employee does your number make you? We've already seen that your birthday suggests you thrive working autonomously under pressure, but when you are in a large group, how do you fit in? If you're the boss, are you a good one? Which fields are likely to be the best for your talents? And which the worst? And what about the male/female divide? Is an 8 female boss more desirable than an 8 male colleague?

Here, we get to grips with your career potential, your needs and 'must-have's for job satisfaction, and your loves and loathes work-wise, hopefully highlighting some areas where there is room for you to adjust your manner around others, to help you achieve what it is you're aiming for.

| 8 | 9 | 1 | 2 | 3 | 4 | 5 | 6 | 7 |

In the marketplace

In business, **8**'s real connection with the inner powers of the astrological sign Scorpio and the functionality of the sign Capricorn come together. Even if you are only just entering your chosen career field, you nevertheless give the impression of being quite a seasoned professional. From the very first day you can compute any weaknesses or identify areas that need developing within a company – regardless of whether big or small – and you will soon prove yourself invaluable in making working life far more efficient for everyone.

When you make assessments, your mind works with extraordinary acuity and impartiality – a combination of gifts which could help you build up any company to its highest potential output, even if it is functioning well below par when you come on board. Very quickly you can establish a reputation as a troubleshooter or a person of ingenuity and charm who is able to take their peers onward and upward, to a new level of success.

NOTHING IS IMPOSSIBLE!

You may be quite traditional in the way you like to see things done. Always fair-minded, you can put together facts and figures with forensic skill to see what is not obvious to anyone else. You have an instinct for business, even if it is your own tiny company of one or two people: you understand what is needed, and will demonstrate amazing feats of human endurance to get something done well – and on time. Focus is never difficult for you.

As long as you feel inspired about what you are doing, you can deal very wisely in the material world and look forward calmly to the moment when you will see the actualization of your ideas hit the marketplace. Even when you are asked to face long periods of struggle, you seem to see a hope about the future that eludes many other people. Any business opportunity should allow you some space to think, for you have the capacity to bring ideas out of darkness – like seeds that germinate in winter – and you actually thrive most when the cupboard seems nearly bare. The best career for you would be something that combines your talents for research and ideas, and it is all the better if there is a degree of experimentation involved in what you are doing. Nothing gives you greater glee than overcoming obstacles, and if anyone tells you that something can't be done, that is your cue to prove them wrong!

Sometimes the number **8** is saddled with too much talk about its powers to earn and create money; but it is certainly the money number, and you will love to earn well and emanate an image of prosperity. Your executive and leadership qualities are likely to give you a career of some distinction, even of fame, and travel may be a part of what you must do in your working life. It is common for an **8** to work in big business, as part of a large corporation, even though a strong degree of autonomy will characterize the way your work life is structured. But even if your own business life is on a smaller scale, you seem certain to become involved with the management of property or a home in some form, for **8** gravitates to real estate in one way or another.

WHERE DOES YOUR LIGHT REALLY SHINE?

Here are some of the qualities that 8s bring to any job:

- The desire for a challenge, and the wish to take something that is weak and make it stronger, may be the biggest talent for an **8**, and subsequently is likely to direct what you choose to do. This leads to questions of marketing and head-hunting, as well as the analysis and repair of weakness at government or social level – but it would fit in with literally any business, in any field, that is in need of a makeover.

- The deeply ingrained sense of moral integrity — which often gets in the way of an **8**'s personal gain — may exhort you to work in a social institution. That ability to weigh and judge what is found wanting, and to offer remedy, is a major asset in a career which depends on any kind of assessment of personnel or evaluation of a project's potential merit. The obvious connection here is with law and accounting, which we will consider in more depth shortly.

- At times, your ability to drive on through a project — with no regard for the depletion of health or the demands of stamina — can astonish other people. That focus, and the power to put personal pain to one side until the job in hand is done, supports any field that expects the absolute limit of human endurance as a matter of course. This power is not only mental but physical, which is why **8** is the number of many outstanding athletes.

- The wish to spoil others – which can actually be slightly controlling, too! – makes you someone who likes to create a feeling of largesse around you work-wise. An **8** boss would never skimp on the quality of the toilet roll or soap in the ladies' room, aware that generating a feeling of everyday luxury makes a happier team. This trait – in many areas – ensures you are respected, and gives you that natural edge of commanding loyalty from those around you.
- Philosophical engagement with life's weighty questions sometimes triggers that interest **8** has in secret societies or elite organizations. In many ways that are not at first obvious, the detective side of your character may come to the fore in your business life – whatever that may be.

All these skills give you a broad portfolio to work with. Your number is, literally, the number of business, so any career is possible for an **8**, and any business will thrive having an **8** in a position of influence.

What can be said is that you *must* find an outlet for your talents for organization and expansive thinking. It is always better not to trust to luck in your work life, so be prepared to study and train at the highest level to give you the tools you need for success in your chosen field. Here are a few areas that may hold a particular appeal ...

The literary world With a thirst for serious knowledge and a love of books, the literary field may have a strong pull for you. **3** is the journalist and **9** writes on a variety of subjects as part of life, but **8** has a very clear appreciation of *literature*. This may manifest in lecturing or teaching about text, or you may become the head of a publishing empire. At the simplest level, success can be found in the world of printing and magazines, in libraries, running research concerns, or working in a position of influence in

7   6   5   4   3   2   1   9   8

newspapers. Overall, though, if books invite you to work with them, it is more likely you may feel interested in writing as an educator or non-fiction compiler than in the realms of drama or romantic fiction.

Property/real estate Property is a real draw-card for the number **8**, and it is a very successful career outlet. Managing property or developing sites so that they have a standout feature, or rescuing buildings which are needy (just like businesses!), will appeal to your talents. You may also find that you like owning property – being a landowner – and that your ideal house, which will become an investment, would be surrounded by some space and acreage, if possible. Either way, your number has an instinct about real estate.

Corporate law This is an area that could be of real interest. No number is a more natural judge or a fairer-minded listener – the two circles of the figure eight representing the wish to see both sides of a discussion. But it is in large-scale business that you flourish, so if the legal world appeals to you, think big! In any business, though, your natural aptitude for legal, logical thinking might find you working with contracts and legalities.

Medicine This may also be a good field for your expression. The research end may particularly appeal, or forensics; and your capacity to stay on your feet longer than anyone should see you through long, late-night shifts in any hospital. However, the natural pull of the **8** to manage and supervise might ultimately point you towards the managerial end of medicine, especially as you have an outstanding ability to handle people and to balance finance with good service. No number is better, either, in an emergency.

Banking and finance Boring as they may be to some, these are perfect fields for you to display your array of talents. There is a selflessness about **8** in business that is naturally suited to major financial advice or investment banking. You are always aware of the needs of the team, and often other people seem to reap more financial reward from your efforts than you do. As long as you are proud of the job, though, you will ultimately feel well-compensated.

This list isn't exhaustive – **8**s can shine in so many different areas – but it does offer a taste of what kinds of field will most appeal to your number.

And for luck?

Whatever your work, you will achieve your maximum potential if you use a name to work with that includes the letters H, Q or Z. Remember this when you are choosing a company name, if you go into business for yourself. It will help, too, for you to optimize your energy and positive attitude, if you decorate your work environment in the bronze/opal/buff hues of fecund autumn. If you are going for an important interview, these colours would make a positive choice in your outfit, as they help you to project yourself in your most powerful and reassuring light.

The 8 female boss

Prowling the lair with acute hearing and an eye for anything not quite right, the **8** female boss is a **force** to be seen. She may be a **dominatrix**, but most of the people she does business with quite like that. She looks expensive, has a **flair** when it comes to exuding the image of **comfortable luxury** to the prospective client reassured by her aura of prosperity, and knows when to let her underlings out on their own, to bring out the best in them. Those who work with her form her guard, like an efficient Roman legion. She is fairly **thick-skinned** about criticism, as long as there's a purpose to the point. If some change is in the interest of the project, she is ready to embrace it.

She can be **cross** with time-wasters but surprisingly **laissez-faire** with her support team – provided she knows

8   9   1   2   3   4   5   6   7

them capable of arduous effort when called upon. She is especially **generous** about sharing praise with all who contributed to a successful venture. But she's **aggressive** if there is a battle to be won: she will prime herself with the accounts figures, learn a few relevant words of another language, research any demographic, and sit up till all hours just to be at fever pitch for a vital meeting in the morning. She probably plays tennis or squash – or power-walks, if that's all time permits – just to meet the mental pressure with **physical stamina**. She will never be caught napping when something needs overseeing; designer-suited, she dominates her domain with **panache**.

And how does she know all those people? Every **8** boss has met the prime minister or the president, the rock star or the entrepreneur; in business, such **contacts** roll off her tongue when she is sure they will cause eyebrows to rise. And don't think she can't **deliver** her promises; she would love to prove you wrong on that score, too!

7   6   5   4   3   2   1   9   8

The 8 male boss

With an **easy air** that belies his **steely control** and his good business sense, the **8** male boss is a **one-off**. He is extremely **fair** with all those who work with him, and, although his personal style may be very much his own, he will never look shabby or wear an ill-fitting suit. His nails are clean and his shoes properly shined, and though he may not look up to the minute, his mind is. Trends are an irrelevance for the **8** man in charge: he **sets his own rules** and makes them work for him. If you want to impress him, show him a **mastery** of every subject relevant to today's meeting or project: it's no more than he would do.

His partner probably understands he'll be late home – **8**'s worst failing is the **inability to put parameters** around their working life. It's likely, in actual fact, that his

| 8 | 9 | 1 | 2 | 3 | 4 | 5 | 6 | 7 |

business and private life **overlap**, for the **8** boss seems to have an unending working day, and only someone who can take that pace could make a permanent relationship with him. But he is **generous** – to his employees and his clients. He won't forget your first name, nor the favourite restaurant of the out-of-town partner he hasn't seen for a year. He **smoothly** manages to orchestrate get-togethers that border on work and social pleasure, and everyone is invited. If a successful deal has just been closed, the champagne will flow. He will never (never!) order house wine for his peers and workforce.

This sense of being **first among equals** allows him to command such **loyalty** from his group. Yes, he can be a **grouch** – especially if someone has repeated a silly mistake or made a gaffe with a client. He may be **frank** to a point of hurt. But his natural style and **showmanship** – all his own – win the day (and everyone) back to him. Advice? Learn everything you can from him!

7   6   5   4   3   2   1   9   8

WORK PROFILE
The 8 female employee

We all know she won't remain just the employee for long. On day one she arrives with her smart Mulberry briefcase and her pashmina flung over her shoulders, with an air that **means business**. This young woman is **determined** to rise. It may not be greed or even a power-hungry attitude that makes this inevitable: she simply doesn't understand being subordinate. Work's more fun when the **responsibility** falls to you. She wants to be in the firing line, and anyone who doesn't like it can work somewhere down the hall. But there won't be many dissenters, because she has **excellent people skills** and **listens** very carefully to what others say. When she takes her iPod away from her ears to answer your query, she is immediately on the case and has the information. Music helps her to concentrate, not escape!

| 8 | 9 | 1 | 2 | 3 | 4 | 5 | 6 | 7 |

Being a **strong character**, the whole office wants to know her business. Who is in her love life? And where does she go when she leaves late? She gets texts and e-mails from a variety of sources, but she is quite **private**, too. Her personal life may be complicated while she gives so much time to her working life. **Career comes first**, until things are moving ... then, career still comes first! She will get her assets together before she gives them away to anyone else. Well, just yet, anyway!

Have a personal crisis? Ask her opinion, because she is a **good counsellor** and gives her time **generously** – but don't rely on her taking your side against the lover who has annoyed you. With **cool impartiality** she will weigh the other party's complaints, too, and if you can't accept her adjudication, don't ask for it. She has a **long memory** and no patience for anyone who refuses sound advice. But such **courage** – to evaluate things so evenly – wins her **plaudits** from above, and promotion very fast!

7 6 5 4 3 2 1 9 8

The 8 male employee

Renowned for his **dry jokes** and expensive shirts (how can he afford them?), the **8** man starting work wants to show everyone what he can do. He is not a sycophant, trying to please everyone – far from it, for he will **tell the truth** mercilessly when asked for it – but he wants to **understand** everyone's role, and make a **broader contribution**. He has a **dynamic** personality and appears to be **in control** right from the start, sprinting from department to department when his skill can add anything useful. He knows the importance of presenting a **successful image**, and is never going to be caught with cheap articles of clothing on show!

Management might be nervous with his arrival, for if anyone is caught sleeping on the job, this **executive-in-the-making** will soon snaffle the best desk and be promoted.

8	9	1	2	3	4	5	6	7

He has an air of **authoritative calm**, and is probably doing a master's degree in the evenings, to gain a better command of the field he's decided to enter. Any subordinate post is a temporary landing stage.

If the females who work with him are attracted, it is because he gives off a certain **air of mystery** without being completely impenetrable. He is **generous** if he joins you for lunch, and an **excellent conversationalist**, because he has read so much, or been to so many interesting places. And perhaps, too, it is a little aphrodisiac that he emanates such **power** and the certainty that he will *be* someone. That he can run well, or play cricket, or dash off a piano sonata, is another intriguing facet. You may never get right to the bottom of him, but if he is working on your patch he will be a **consistent**, hard-working and **dependable** team-mate who is prepared to sacrifice personal brownie points for the sake of the wider unit. Just don't imagine he'll be at the foot of any ladder for long!

7   6   5   4   3   2   1   9   8

Ideal world or cruel world?
Best and worst jobs ...

IN AN IDEAL WORLD
Best job for an 8 female: Senior secret-services boss
(delving into international secrets, protecting her team,
scope to master several serious skills, can't pass the buck,
equal footing with men)

Best job for an 8 male: Surgeon in busy hospital who has
risen to become chief of staff (challenge of life-and-
death aspect of work combined with keeping funding
and functionality at a premium)

IN A CRUEL WORLD
Worst job for an 8 female: Small-charity worker whose
hands are tied trying to generate enough funds for
expansion (desperate frustration at bureaucratic
injustices make it intolerable)

Worst job for an 8 male: Local councillor who can't rise
above the small-town attitude of his peers (vision and
energy destroyed by the reality of old-fashioned views)

8'S CHILDHOOD

Seeing the way a number expresses itself in someone very young is fascinating, for the tendencies and responses are all in their infancy – and yet plain to see. Some facets of a number's power need to be grown into, and take time to reveal how they will be dealt with by the developing character. Sometimes the strength of a number can be a frustration when we're young.

If looking back on your own childhood through the lens of your number, you should discover – with considerable humour and irony – a renewed understanding of some of the difficulties or excitements you experienced. Or, if you have a child who is also an **8**, you may learn something more useful; it is an advantage to understand the qualities

7   6   5   4   3   2   1   9   8

a number exudes over an awakening personality, especially in relation to talents and career strengths, as it might save a lot of frustrations. You'll be able to appreciate the positive traits, and handle negative ones more sympathetically.

Here, we take a detailed look at what it's like to be a child bearing your number. But what about the other numbers? Perhaps you have a child who is a **3**, and you'd like to know what that means? Or maybe you'd like to gain insight into friends' and siblings' childhoods, to see if it sheds any light on the people they have become today? A short profile is given for each number, along with advice for an **8** parent on dealing with other-number offspring.

Just as your own parents would have discovered when you were a child, the hardest thing with an **8** child is helping them to find fruitful expression for their energy and strength of will, and their wish to balance everything. Self-discipline will show them the way forward eventually, but harmony must be the goal for the parents of an **8** …

8   9   1   2   3   4   5   6   7

he young 8

A child born on the 8th, 17th or 26th of the month is a young executive in the making. Careful with their pocket money, and aware of the value of work and chores, an **8** child is ready to contribute to their own upkeep. Even when still at school, these children have a canny nose for what will make good business – and yet, they are outstandingly generous and hard-working, prepared to learn everything it will take to succeed in this life, and ready to share the fruits of their success with anyone dear to them.

Children born with an **8** birthday like to have charge of their own finances, and to be given scope to do 'grown-up' activities – organizing their own parties, for instance, and making arrangements for outings with their friends. If they want something badly, they will work out a plan for earning extra cash to achieve that goal themselves –

rather than wheedling an extra gift out of Mum, or batting their eyelids at Dad.

8 children have impressive bouts of strength and energy – long periods where they can concentrate to achieve whatever fascinates them – so don't be surprised if a project keeps them outdoors from dawn till dusk, or at their desk way beyond the dinner bell. But they are mentally reflective and wise, too. To harmonize all things – very much like a **6** – is their chief interest, and they will be irritated by dissent between siblings and parents if it seems to be a repeated pattern. Wise beyond their years, they always see both sides of an argument, so parents who ask them to choose sides, beware! An **8** makes good judgements, and even before they have reached the age of ten they have a sense of what is fair and what is morally right.

As the number rules the musical octave, many **8** children are extremely gifted musicians and have a delicate ear and a fine sense of rhythm. It is this last that suggests

8's toys

Running shoes • MP3 player • Xylophone, piano or guitar • Tennis racket • Book club membership (always buy good-quality books for them to keep) • Jewellery • Atlas • Mystery-based board games • Telescope • Encyclopedia • Lockable diary

they may be good at sport, as it takes innate timing and physical balance – along with training and rigour – to perfect complex physical skills. If they are particularly sociable, with perhaps a **6** or **3** as their LIFE number (*see page 214*), they will excel at team games; but if they have a preponderance of '**1**' letters ('A's and 'S's) in their name, or a LIFE number of **1**, they are more likely to prefer the loneliness of the long-distance runner or the distance swimmer.

But, mentally agile and very bright, **8**s also enjoy philosophical concepts and debates, and they will relish being given mysterious or imponderable subjects to reflect on, *especially* concerning politics or religious ideas. **8**s are proud, sometimes stubborn, and self-reliant, and they like to research things carefully for themselves. As long as they are not bored, you will find an **8** child on the internet or with their head in a book, or watching television pro- grammes that educate and broaden their thinking. They often seem above the reach of their own peer group.

An **8** child is always reaching for a balanced life, just like numbers **2** and **6** – who are, of course, also quite musical. They do not like injustice and will speak up if they feel one person is constantly favoured over another, or if someone is frequently denied, or treated with unkindness. It is less from a tender heart – as in the case of **6** – and more from a philosophical awareness that such distinction and preferment is wrong. An **8**'s parents must learn to be pragmatic when their child sometimes pulls in the oppo- site direction from them. Their moves and actions are the product of their own thought rather than what is imbued as a habit; but, though they are independent, **8**s are also very loyal and supportive to those they love, and instinct makes them look at the other side of a story, or fight for an underdog.

If an **8** finds a friend dejected or a parent overburdened, they will do their childish best to rally them with sensible words and philosophical ideals. **2**s, **6**s and **9**s also understand this care of others well, but an **8** child is more driven than these numbers, and more determined to redress the balance of inequality or injustice.

School may be a mixed experience for them, wanting to get to the relevant points of what they wish to do as quickly as possible. But an **8** will go on with self-education throughout life. A philosophical and material balance is where they are headed – ideally!

The 1 child

This resourceful child has a different way of thinking, and will stand to one side and evaluate things without pressure. Repeat Grandma's sound advice on any subject to a **1** under the age of six, and they'll simply ask, 'Why?' Ignoring the social expectation to conform, **1** children often make us laugh with surprise.

A **1** child is tough and active – an inquisitive soul who wants to get on with things and not be held in check by others, however wise the parental eye might be. Stubborn and impatient, **1**s frequently suffer by questioning – though not from rudeness – the authority of a parent or teacher. **1**s break down tradition and find new ideas to form a fresh understanding of the world we're in. Your **1** child needs careful handling: a bright mind bursting with interest and disinclined to authority needs subtle direction. If **1** children dominate their friends and talk over their family it can make them socially inept and unable to co-operate in love relationships later in life, leading to loneliness rather than just self-reliance.

A **1**'s greatest challenge is to learn to live in a social world and understand that they are not inevitably right. To foster a **1**'s unique personality and avoid insensitivity to others, let them behave like an adult. This confidence a **1** child will ably repay. **1** children suffer from being misunderstood, as they're often so happy in their private hours and so demanding of having their own time that they may not learn to express their need for others. The seeds are sown early as to how to approach another person for signs of affection, and a wise **8** parent will know perfectly how to 'invade' their **1** child's space without imbalance, offering good counsel at the appropriate moment. You won't cosset your independent **1** too much, knowing that they would simply break free.

7   6   5   4   3   2   1   9   8

The 2 child

All children born on the 2nd or 20th need affection and a peaceful environment to grow up in. Those born on the 11th or 29th are a little different, being master number **11**s with **2** as the denominator, and they have an old head on young shoulders from the start. But even they – for all their drive toward excitement and adventure – will be happiest if their home life is mostly secure and tranquil.

These highly sensitive and intuitive children know what you will say before you say it. They are also dreamy and process ideas in their sleep, waking to instinctive and wise solutions to their problems. But they are vulnerable, and need reassuring more than most numbers. They are acutely sensitive to criticism, feeling that all comments are proof that they're not quite good enough, so you need to deliver your words with tact and an awareness of their needs.

| 8 | 9 | 1 | 2 | 3 | 4 | 5 | 6 | 7 |

2 children are talented artists, actors, dancers and/or musicians: they know how others *feel*. A **2** child prefers to support friends and family as often as possible, and this can make them a doormat ready to be walked on unless those they live with are alert to their inclinations. If the **2** is an **11**, the wish to help out will be very strong indeed, but these children also have a finely tuned moral sense and will be offended by injustice – especially against them! Don't dish out judgement until you have all the facts.

2s are good healers and can make others feel better – even from their earliest years. Knowing when to cuddle or touch and when to be quiet, they often have a stillness that works miracles around the sick, the sad and the elderly. An **8** parent will respect this, always ready with praise, appreciating their **2** child's need for inner calm and harmony, like their own. They have a similar feeling for what is right and wrong, and you will enjoy the sensitive affection and support you receive from your gentle, intelligent, musical **2**.

7   6   5   4   3   2   1   9   8

The 3 child

From the cradle, **3**s hold parties and like to mix with other children. They have a capacity to laugh and precipitate laughter, even when things go a little wrong. **3** children are like the reappearing sun after rain, and their energies can be restorative for everyone. Creative and playful, nothing keeps them low for long.

Like a juggler keeping plates and balls in the air, **3**s have several activities and talents on the go from the start. This can be a problem, however: making decisions is hard for them, and they need a wise older counsellor who can talk out the options and give them room to think. Even then, a decision once reached can always be changed – and a **3** child will find a way to run in several directions at one time.

Keep your **3** busy with lots of artistic activities, using colours and textures – right from babyhood – to open their eyes to what they can do. Even before the age of ten a strong personal taste will begin to develop – and it may not be the same as their parents'. Using up their flow of energy on a multitude of tasks will be demanding on both parents, but the **3** child does give a great deal back in return.

3s are talkers and have a witty repartee, even when tiny: you'll be surprised at what you hear from them sometimes, and will wonder where it came from. Naturally gifted at PR, they will talk you around when you are set against one of their wishes, but you will need to direct them now and again or nothing will ever be finished! An **8** parent with a **3** child must give them freedom to experiment, and try not to control them too much or be irritated if they are disorganized, or chatter wildly. Be wise and kind, and don't worry if they rush about without your directed purpose: they have a way of coming back smiling.

The 4 child

Surprisingly insecure and in need of praise, these children are reliable and hard-working and want to do well. They are their own worst critics at times, second only to number **7** children, and they glow when appreciated. They are happiest with family around them – even extended members – and often prefer holidays in familiar places. That said, they can be very quiet and self-sufficient when required, for they concentrate well.

These are organized children who won't cope well if their parents aren't as organized as they are! Never lose a school form or an item from their games kit on a crucial day, as this will cause them serious panic. They like to have material possessions around them because this bolsters their feeling of security, and will manage their pocket money well, content to do odd jobs and chores to gain this reward.

4s love the earth and buildings. They will treasure a patch of garden given them to tend, or a garden house they can extend or build outright. If they are born on the 22nd, rather than the 4th, 13th or 31st, they will truly have architectural talents, and may follow design as a career later. All **4** children, though, are handy at craft work and excellent at projects which require intelligence combined with method to get something done. They hate being late and don't admire tardiness in others, either.

As children, **4**s are loyal and dependable to family and friends, and are more patient than many numbers. They will make light of complex tasks, but they need to be allowed to do things in their own way. An **8** parent will be proud of the care and order their **4** child takes, but perhaps think them slightly unimaginative. **4**s feel responsible to others, though, which you'll encourage. Your inspiring direction and their good focus blend well, and you will respect their tenacity. The relationship will grow closer with time.

7 6 5 4 3 2 1 9 8

The 5 child

Unable to be confined or sit still, a **5** child is bursting with curiosity. Very sociable and happy to be on the move, these adventurous youngsters have much in common with **1**s, but are more willing to work in a team, and good at picking up on other people's ideas, only to improve them.

From their first few words, **5** children have good memories and a facility for speech – they speak and learn quickly, and can pick up more than one language. Even more physical than **1**s (although the two numbers are alike in this), they are excellent at sport or physical co-ordination. They chatter, are full of energy, and like to play to an audience. But most importantly, **5** children love to be free – to explore, laze, hunt, create, discover and travel. Take your **5** child away on holiday and they quickly make friends with others, and acquire a taste for foreign places. They will

8   9   1   2   3   4   5   6   7

even experiment with different food, if you're lucky.

5s find a reason to slip away if they're bored with adult company – so don't be offended. Their minds can pursue several streams of active interest, so they need a great deal of amusement to stretch them. This adventurous spirit can be a worry to their family sometimes and, indeed, **5**s need to understand house rules about asking first, or telling someone where they're off to. The difficulty is that **5** children usually don't want to explain themselves to anyone.

The test for a **5**'s parent is to set their child constructive challenges that will vent their curiosity in good ways. **5**s will pick up technology and music (other forms of language, in a sense) quickly, but they don't like dull routine work – which will irritate a **4** sibling if they have one. An **8** parent of a **5** child will need to give them freedom to do their own thing, and will frown on their restlessness and noise; but you will admire their imaginative talent and creative energy. You'll need to be patient, though!

The 6 child

Here's a young soul in need of a peaceful haven, just like a
2, but a **6** will literally feel ill if there is dissension around
them. Always wanting to beautify their surroundings and
make pretty presents for Mum, these talented, sensitive
children have many gifts for creative expression. They will
also nurse the sick cat or anyone who needs gentle kindness, but are not always robust themselves, and should be
sheltered from bad weather or aggressive viruses.

As children, **6**'s musical talents should emerge – and
they often have beautiful speaking or singing voices. They
are also the peacemakers of the family – natural creators
of balance and harmony. Give them a free hand with their
bedroom and their flower garden, and be ready to learn
from them. Both boys and girls usually make good cooks
when they are older, too, so time spent in the kitchen won't

8   9   1   2   3   4   5   6   7

be wasted. Birthday presents that foster their good eye — a camera or set of art tools — will usually fit them well.

Despite being sensitive to others and quite intuitive, **6** as a child is a little shy and needs drawing out — especially if there has been much change in their young life, because **6** children need stability and like to remain a tiny bit traditional. They become very attached to their home. But if their family life is unconventional they will ultimately adjust, because they offer their family a lot of love, and like to be shown love in return. Even the boys have a feminine side which in no way calls their gender into question.

Good at school and almost as well-organized as **4**s, this is a number which needs time to grow into itself: **6**s are enormously talented. An **8** parent will be kind and appreciative towards their artistic, sensitive **6** child. When you need a friend to listen, support, encourage and back *you* up, you will often find unsuspected reservoirs of strength in this interesting child.

7   6   5   4   3   2   1   9   8

The 7 child

This is a child with a focused mind and a strongly developed critical sense. A **7** child is perceptive and, sometimes, disarmingly quiet. They will often prefer adult company, as their peers will probably seem too young and underdeveloped to them. Wise and difficult to know well, these are children with a serious cast to their intelligent minds.

The fact that a **7** child can sit quietly and contemplate things deeply should not imply that they are introverted: quite the opposite. A **7** will grow into a very good host as long as the company appeals, and they have a lovely sense of humour, apparent from their earliest years – even if it does sometimes find expression at others' expense. They will rarely be rude, but certainly have a good understanding of all that has been said – and what has not been. Listen to their impressions of the people they deal with!

| 8 | 9 | 1 | 2 | 3 | 4 | 5 | 6 | 7 |

All **7**s as children have an inward reluctance to accept other people's ideas automatically – rather like **1**s – but there is a special propensity to independence in a child born on the 16th. This is the number of someone who finds it difficult asking for what they want – someone who often feels as though they haven't been consulted as to their own wishes. And all **7**s certainly have definite ideas about what to believe.

7 children should be told the truth on virtually all matters; they will know if they are being deceived, and will respect being treated as an adult in any case – which is an **8** parent's natural inclination, too. Even *you* may find their maturity a little unnerving, but you will respect your **7** child's strength and drive to excel in what they like. Though different – a **7** child wanting to retire more into personal space – your numbers appreciate each other, and a **7** child gives any parent much to be proud of, both academically and in terms of humanitarian feelings.

7   6   5   4   3   2   1   9   8

The 9 child

Here is a person born for the theatre, or to travel the world and befriend everyone. **9**s have an expansive view, and don't like to be restricted. With a good head for science and the arts, there are many career directions a **9** may take, so parents will have their work cut out trying to help them choose. However, because the number **9** is like a mirror, with every number added to it reducing again to that same number (for example: 5+9 = 14, and 1+4 = 5), **9** children are able to take on the feelings of just about anyone, which is why they are so artistic and good at drama and writing.

From their first years in school it will be clear a **9** child has a wonderful dry sense of humour and a taste for the unusual. **9** children are not often prejudiced and seem to be easy-going – though they are sensitive to the atmosphere around them, picking up vibes like a sponge. If you

8   9   1   2   3   4   5   6   7

speak to them harshly they will take it seriously, and are protective of others who seem to be hurt in this way too.

9s have a delicate relationship with their parents, but particularly with the father figure. A **9** girl will want to idolize her dad, and will feel desperately disappointed if circumstances are against this, while a **9** boy may wish to emulate his father – and yet they often grow up without enough input from this important person, who is busy or away. A **9** child must be wise ahead of their time, and so this lesson is thrown at them in one guise or another.

The **8** parent of a **9** child understands how to be hospitable, allowing a stream of their friends through the door. Your **9** child appreciates your warmth and feeling for their friends, and recognizes your pride in them and engagement in their hobbies, rewarding you with affection and kindness. Grown-ups from the start (like you), their philosophical mind and willingness to keep the peace fills you with admiration – but don't control or organize them too rigorously!

7 6 5 4 3 2 1 9 8

8 AT PLAY

We have discovered how your number expresses
itself through your character in relation to your
family and your general personality, what instinctive
reactions go with your number in everyday
situations, and how it might shape your career path
and colour your childhood. But every day our DAY
number also influences the way we respond to the
social world around us. So, what can it say about our
leisure hours? Is yours a number that even allows
itself to relax? (Well, you probably already have
some answers to this one!) What can your number
reveal about the way you like to spend your time,
or how you achieve pleasure outside of duty?

8	9	1	2	3	4	5	6	7

Over the next few pages we take a look at what makes you tick, as an **8**, when you are unwinding – and how **8**s prefer to fill their time, if given a choice. Let's see whether you're typical in this respect ... And who knows – if you haven't already tried all the activities and pastimes mentioned, maybe you'll get a few ideas about what to put on your list for next time!

The 8 woman at play

Looking back over the significant traits of the **8** character to this point, you will see a recurring theme of a busy soul with a restless mind and a need to be doing something: **8**s are *doers* rather than observers. The **8** woman in her leisure time is always moving forwards. A week off may see you start writing that novel, or shopping around for a further education course; or you may even browse for other business opportunities. An **8** girl knows how to turn hobbies and passions into pocket money, right from the word 'go'. That urge to put something on paper, or make a splash on the canvas, amounts to quite a strenuous force to be useful, motivated, excited by something. You will definitely unwind – but the nature of that 'unwinding' is never idle. This is what makes you overwhelm your more chilled-out or (you might say) plodding associates!

| 8 | 9 | 1 | 2 | 3 | 4 | 5 | 6 | 7 |

Being an entertaining companion, you make use of your well-stocked mind to amuse your friends. Chit-chat time may be combined with the wish to go water-skiing or walking, but you're a good listener on the move, and combine the feat of offering wise words on a love rift while preparing for the next half-marathon. And, you have a friend to share each and every one of your very different activities, so social hours are crammed with a variety of people and places. There'll be the platonic lover you go to concerts with, and the older women with whom you discuss literature. Sundays before lunch might be reserved for the ex-boyfriend with whom you still have a part-time business interest, or the ex-husband whose cat you mind perfectly amiably; having arranged the demise in an impartial way that suited you, you see no need to cut off the interesting characters who have peppered your past.

There will always be leisure time for sport in an **8** lady's life: if you are only watching the Olympics, you know you're

7   6   5   4   3   2   1   9   8

being lazy! If someone asks you to go sailing, or cycling in France, you can pack very quickly – though you are likely to take some work away with you, too – either because you're stressed and overworked all the time, or because you can't bear getting too far behind. You'll take school books on a plane ride to a short holiday break, and get texts sent to your cell phone with updates of the World Cup results for the first coffee break at the conference. You are happy balancing work and pleasure in each hand.

Preferred hobbies might include writing, playing music and reading. The researcher's mind is never still in an **8** woman: digging up interesting information gives you a buzz, and becomes your way to relax. Even a very arts-inspired **8** will have a feeling for science – mainly for the research aspects of it. Contenders for your favourite television stations are likely to include Discovery, or the Arts channel, and you also like reading about everything in the past that remains unsolved.

Cooking may or may not be one of your priorities – though, with your reverence for the working brunch, the coffee morning or the tea break, it's likely that you indulge in a little baking – but you are very happy to be a host to your friends at dinner. Both male and female **8s**' hobbies include restaurant-hopping, and, as **8s** love luxury as much as breathing, fine hotels also show up in colour on their personal planners. There is no word that translates as 'budget' when leisure time takes you to one of these!

Whether you're going out on the town or out of town, you only know where to find venues of quality. Men who want to be part of your personal life will need to bear this in mind – but, if you can afford it, you will treat everyone yourself. **8** girls don't expect their men to spoil them on their away-days, preferring the balance to be the other way around!

The 8 man at play

Happiest spoiling the people he loves, the **8** man uses his leisure hours to enhance someone's life. Others may think this sounds too good to be true, but – rather like the unselfish **6** man – you are generous with both your wallet (budget allowing) and your time, and if you have a day off you will use it to lift any deserving soul's spirits. Of course, getting the day off is the tough one: you are likely to be taking phone calls on holiday or in the restaurant – never meaning to be rude to your guests, however! But when you do arrange a balance of free hours, you are always looking after other people's wishes. And you are such a stylish host!

Ever met a man who has renovated a French chateau or restored some lovely gardens in a period property, largely so he can ask his friends to join him there? That

8   9   1   2   3   4   5   6   7

man is likely to be an **8**. Or had a postcard from the man on holiday in Tuscany, detouring via the Veneto just to pick up a motorbike or a kitchen sink for his cousin or daughter-in-law? Just see if he hasn't an **8** birthday! With effortless grace and a seamless transition from one course to the other, the **8** man is the orchestrator of the perfect wedding feast or the delicious dirty weekend in splendid comfort. You use your money, connections and largesse in your free time, to treat your friends.

When not playing out the role of a scaled-down Nelson Rockefeller (birthday 8th July), you'll be jogging or golfing (well, somebody must!), or enjoying a drive in your comfortable (and quietly quick) car, with the sound system on. Music and movement feed your soul, and you are aware of the need for a balance of health and fitness with career stamina. You may even have won the local tennis tournament – and we can be sure you got there with forty per cent talent and sixty per cent determination and graft. If anyone wants to run you to ground, they'll have to get fit with you.

You have an interest in property, and may pursue this at your leisure. This, again, is where business and holiday merge, for your philosophy plainly is that you understand the need to love the work you do so that it becomes a pleasure – and, having arranged your business life to suit yourself, you are in control of your own hours. It is hard to imagine you lying on a beach with your mind adrift, but you have read, seen, considered many things, and can take pleasure in abstract interests which defeat other people's imagination. You take your pleasure everywhere, inside your head.

With that sense of balance and rhythm that is also found, to some degree, in a **6**, the **8** man may sing well or play the piano, and enjoys history and art – though you're not obsessed about becoming a perfectionist, as a **7** would be. Dipping into a panoply of interests, you are ready to try a dozen things before you will scorn them, because your open mind demands that you should do so. Ultimately, as with an **8** woman, your ranging mind is the gateway to your pleasure, and you are flexible. Those who share your private hours must see free time differently – working holidays and research trips being more a reality than spa time. And, like the **8** lady, you shall have music wherever you go.

8 IN LOVE

Love: it's what we all want to know about. What's your style as a lover? And your taste – where does that run? Do you want a partner who allows you to take subtle control? Or would you rather have a love in your life who can be equally outgoing and support *you* at times? You are discerning, even though you enjoy a diverse range of people, but are you too much of a workaholic to enter fully into your love life?

Our first task is to consider how you see others as potential partners, and what you are likely to need from them. Why are you attracted to someone in the first place? This is where we begin ... But then you might like to pass the book across to your other half (if you have one), for the second subject of discussion is: why are *they* attracted to *you*? What does it mean to have an **8** lover?

Telltale traits of the 8 lover

- Can fall in love deeply
- Loyal, but may forget to express loving sentiments to those closest
- Needs a partner to allow them to balance work responsibilities and personal time
- Very generous
- Gets on with many people
- Charismatic
- Individualistic character makes a vivid impression on others

How do you do?
AN 8 IN ATTRACTION

With an air of grandeur and the ability to stand out from the crowd, you find it easy talking to most people thanks to an instinctive sense of confidence about who you are yourself. That said, **8** loves to form an attraction for someone who has a little gloss or shine about them. Picking up signals through a kind of osmosis, you somehow gravitate towards the most interesting and extraordinary people in a room – though it is rarely someone's visual appearance that attracts you alone.

The person who steals your imagination is the one who has a fascinating life story, or a position of some esteem within their own sphere; without contriving it outwardly, **8** finds the talented, well-connected, important person in a gathering. But you may also be attracted to a potential lover through the most intangible qualities – someone who simply seems fascinating or diverse, or who plays the piano magnificently. An **8** in love rarely chooses the simple path to joy!

The full monty

Although outward beauty is not a necessary requisite in love, you are nonetheless appreciative of the aesthetic, and you will certainly notice anyone whose style of dress is quietly expensive – though not vulgar. **8** desires quality: the man in the corner who is dressed with discretion, but wears a shirt that the cognoscenti recognize as classic and expensive; or the woman who is wearing an understated plain-coloured garment made of the finest fabric and cut to perfection. It's not the prominence of the cheekbone or the exquisite line of the jaw, so much as the inner radiance and outward emanation of authority and strength that will captivate your heart.

And, **8** loves someone who seems sexy and fit physically. For you, beauty is a whole package – a good mind and polished exterior must go together. However, you are not necessarily sold on someone who has money to offer, because **8** is willing – intentionally or not – to take on the burden of the earning. You are ambitious about the kind of partner you want, but it is not an ambition that demands a moneyed lover. Social warmth and experience of life will do better.

You will never form a strong or lasting relationship with anyone whose mind is not fertile. You expect – and get – a partner with whom you can talk and really explore life's mysteries. You may not be immune to a lovely face or body every time, but if this alone is what a relationship comes to be about, it won't last for you – and you certainly won't repeat the mistake. Anyone you are deeply attracted to must enhance your life, and elevate your feelings. You are ready to improve yourself in some way, to gain the lover you hunt – even to the extent of a 'Groundhog Day'-style reuse of your time and energy. **8** loves to earn their lover, just as they are ready to earn everything of value in life.

Go easy

8s attract much admiration from diverse lovers, partly because they are enigmatic. Your deep soul and interesting blend of the intellectual and the spiritual make you a mystery to others, but you may need to curb your openness and honesty in the early stages of attraction. Never meaning to give offence, you are inclined to call something as you see it, and it can take time for those around you to understand that this kind of statement and observation from you bears no malice.

Give a dawning love affair time to adjust to you – to

the dynamism and independent mind that you have. You exude great mental vitality and sometimes unleash a torrent of energy in your wake, but this can be overwhelming to a love relationship still in its infancy: tiny seedlings need time to grow without being crowded. Retreat, if possible, into that more secretive and enigmatic side of your character that wants a little gentle teasing out from your partner. 8's sheer forcefulness and strength sometimes obliterates a lover's own contribution.

Looking for adventure

Once your heart is pledged to that multi-faceted lover who can sing, and balance Schubert with The Clash, whose mind has been broadly educated and who can show you a healthy degree of their own independence alongside an appreciation of your ability to floor them with surprise events, you will expect them to accommodate your many friends of both sexes, as well as the spill of your work life into your domestic space. An **8** is not stimulated by a jealous lover, but irritated by it; and you may simply feel your beloved *knows* how much you care, or how you register what they do for you. Try not to be too busy for romance – because, when you do make time for it, you upstage all others. An inventive and boundless imagination gives you the edge (in courtship) over virtually anyone else. Don't neglect to deploy this wonderful skill from time to time!

So what are you looking for, as an **8**, in a love affair? A complex love, who has enough sense of themselves to do without you when they must, but to make you the pillar they lean on when you're there; someone who tolerates your music collection, and accepts the eccentricities of your working life; a person who sees that you would like to make a better place – and even that there might just be a way to create more of a paradise on earth – but who is willing to sacrifice some leisure time to be with you. You don't want Mr or Ms Average, but you won't offer anything banal or run-of-the mill in return, either. Love with an **8** is an adventure story ... so now hand the book over to your lover, and they can find out what they've let themselves in for.

To have and to hold?

LOVING A NUMBER 8

If you have fallen for the charms and sheer magnitude of an **8**'s personality, you had better be ready to demonstrate some independence of both spirit and action. An **8** may love you to bits, but they are never going to be there all the time. **8**, in fact, must learn to balance rest time with their constant striving to *achieve*. Their relationships frequently suffer from a shortage of time for relaxation, for **8**s rarely rest on their laurels, and are sometimes hurtful by appearing to prioritize other people or demands over a lover or family. (In fact, family means the world to an **8**, but few people know this.)

This powerhouse character is, of course, part of what you are drawn to: outshining all competition with their sheer force of will and ethical, personable exterior, an **8** walks in the room and appears to take quiet control – and what can be sexier? This is someone who appears to have a long memory for other people's interests and troubles, and who makes time for everyone from any walk of life. They are as personable with the hairdresser as with the pop diva, and as likely to be on first-name terms with the postman or the prime minister. Riveting stuff for any admirer. An **8** is aware that who you know can be very important, but equally recognizes that everyone is important in their own way. This is an endearing side to their character, and makes them very attractive to the opposite sex.

Excess baggage

Bear in mind, though, if you have your heart set on an **8**, that they come with some emotional baggage. Even a young **8** has family history to deal with and any number of (captivating!) skeletons in their closet. Nothing with an

8 is exactly as it seems and, although your **8** love doesn't mean to be obtuse or anything less than honest, there are just so many labyrinthine paths that loop around their personal love garden that you may feel it takes forever to get to the centre of it all. You may even want to give up! A previous brief engagement or even marriage may emerge, or a tangled family life with siblings who are a surprise; **8** is deep for a reason, and has become a deep-thinking philosopher through some personal pain or strange circumstances.

Your **8** needs love and affection to soften out their hard corners, and admiration from someone they trust is likely to bring out their sweetness, too. But be patient getting there: an **8** is very testing, fitting no exact blueprints and conforming to no absolute norms. They are spiritual but also rational, impartial but also strongly feeling, impatient of mistakes but also a patient and willing tutor. Such paradoxes can confuse mortals who love them!

7 6 5 4 3 2 1 9 8

What lies beneath

And sexually? Let me not give the impression that an **8** boy or girl is all work and no play! Having made the point that an **8** is physical and often sporty, **8**s love good physical relationships and have a no-holds-barred policy about sex – even though they can be quite traditional and morally upright in most ways.

An **8** can be experimental and surprisingly adventurous about their sensual life – less so than a **5**, perhaps, but with at least as much imagination and willing spark as a **1**. Be prepared to discover some of that deep quietness in some strange places – and be prepared to be spoiled with your **8** lover. Just make sure you can negotiate some free time to allow the space to enjoy it. Take that phone off the hook, or disconnect the doorbell – otherwise, the rest of day-to-day life may encroach on this very private and passionate territory.

8   9   1   2   3   4   5   6   7

For marriage and love, your **8** can be oh so loyal and true to you; but the rollercoaster ride cuts in for other reasons. If you take on an **8**, be prepared for feast and famine at times, hard work and patches of uncertainty. In a lifetime, an **8** can make and lose more than one fortune, and a partner's role may be precarious through the rougher times. If you have faith – as well you might – in your **8**'s capacity to recover from adversity and replenish the fountain of hope over and again, you should have an extraordinary life, where you see and experience more than most people are capable of in their imagination.

8 in love

Turn-ons:

♥ ✔ A lover who shows faith in your ability
♥ ✔ Someone with a musical ear and a love of the whole canvas of life
♥ ✔ A person with a bright mind and enough self-possession not to be clingy
♥ ✔ Someone with a sense of humour – essential!

Turn-offs:

♥ ✘ A chatterer to no purpose
♥ ✘ Someone who is unconcerned with politics and broader issues
♥ ✘ Anyone who is completely narcissistic, or who loves your money but is greedy in its use
♥ ✘ A lover who can't share you with many other demands

8   9   1   2   3   4   5   6   7

8'S COMPATIBILITY

In this weighty section you have the tools to find out how well you click with all the other numbers in matters of the heart, but also when you have to work or play together too. Each category opens with a star-ratings chart, showing you – at a glance – whether you're going to encounter plain sailing or stormy waters in any given relationship. First up is love: if your number matches up especially well with the person you're with, you will appreciate why certain facets of your bond just seem to slot together easily.

But, of course, we're not always attracted to the people who make the easiest relationships for us, and if you find that the one you love rates only one or two stars, don't

7 6 5 4 3 2 1 9 8

give in! Challenges are often the 'meat' of a love affair – and all difficulties are somewhat soothed if you both share a birthday number in common, even if that number is derived from the *total* of the birth date rather than the actual DAY number. In other words, if your partner's LIFE number is the same as your DAY number, you will feel a pull towards each other which is very strong, even if the DAY numbers taken together have some wrinkles in their match-up. You will read more about this in the pages that follow the star chart.

The charts also include the master numbers **11** and **22**: these bring an extra dimension to relationships for those whose birth-number calculations feature either of these numbers at any stage. (For example, someone with a DAY number of **2** may be born on the 29th: 2+9 = **11**, and 1+1 = **2**. This means you should read the compatibility pairings for your number with both a **2** and an **11**.)

Sometimes the tensions that come to the surface in

love relationships are excellent for business relationships instead: the competitiveness that can undermine personal ties can accelerate effectiveness in working situations. We'll take a look at how other numbers match up with yours in vocational situations. And, when it comes to friends, you'll see why not all of your friendships are necessarily a smooth ride ...

In all matters – whether love, work or friendship – you will probably discover that the best partnerships you make involve an overlap of at least one number that you share in common. A number **8** attracts other number **8**s in various close ties throughout life.

NOTE: To satisfy your curiosity, ALL numbers are included in the star charts, so that you can check the compatibility ratings between your friends, co-workers and loved ones – and see why some relationships may be more turbulent than others!

7   6   5   4   3   2   1   9   8

Love

YOUR **LOVE** COMPATIBILITY CHART

	1	2	3	4	5
With a 1	★★★★	★★★★★	★★	★★★	★★★★
With a 2	★★★★★	★★★★	★★★	★★★★★	★
With a 3	★★	★★★	★★★★★	★★	★★★★
With a 4	★★★	★★★★★	★★	★★★★	★★
With a 5	★★★★★	★	★★★★	★★	★★★
With a 6	★★★	★★★★	★★★★	★★★	★★
With a 7	★★★★★	★★	★★★	★★★★★	★★★
With an 8	★★★★	★★★★	★★★★★	★★★	★★★
With a 9	★★★	★★★	★★★★★	★★	★★★
With an 11	★★★★	★★★★	★★	★★★★★	★★
With a 22	★★★★	★★★★★	★★★	★★★★	★★★★

6	7	8	9	11	22
★★★	★★★★★	★★★★	★★★	★★★★	★★★★
★★★★	★★	★★★★	★★★	★★★★	★★★★★
★★★★	★★★	★★★★★	★★★★★	★★	★★★
★★★	★★★★★	★★★	★★	★★★★★	★★★★
★★	★★★	★★★	★★★	★★	★★★★
★★★★	★	★★★	★★★★★★	★★★★	★★★★
★	★★★	★★★★	★★★	★★★★	★★★★★
★★★	★★★★	★★★	★★	★★★★★	★★★★
★★★★	★★★	★★	★★★	★★★★	★★★
★★★★	★★★★	★★★★★	★★★★	★★	★★★★★
★★★★	★★★★★	★★★★	★★★	★★★★★	★★

7	6	5	4	3	2	1	9	8

8 in love with a 1   ★★★★

This is a relationship with at least occasional fireworks. You are both aggressive in a positive way, and you like to make things happen, so this allows for the chance of a really dynamic bond with much mental activity and physical pleasure in the offing. Of course, there is also the chance that you may become rivals! It very much depends on whether you are attracted to one another in a narcissistic fashion, or simply admire the qualities you each exude. Co-operation is the key point.

When you harness your considerable mental acuity and drive, you have the kind of combined potential that most businesses would dream of – which is one reason why you are an excellent business team (see also page 182). In love, however, you are likely to bring out the best and the worst in each other, because it is of no account which of you is the female and which the male, since both numbers are dominant. You can either decide to join each other, and let your talents work in unison, or destroy each other with too much competitive energy.

Naturally, this electrical kind of attraction – with sparks flying in all directions – is great for sex! Your physical magnetism may be just what got you started, and it will probably go on working well even when other facets of your relationship become rocky. The basic problem is that you want to take control of **1**'s ideas and move them outwards to a broader audience, but, in doing so, your **1** may feel pressured to compromise their individuality. Also, it may frustrate them that their charismatic **8** tries to do all of the jobs and become all things to all people – leaving no time for them personally. And, there are definitely clashes of ego ahead between you.

But the good bits are very good. You both have diverse interests, speak your mind, and have an intensity about you – especially when it comes to getting projects started. You are generous and love seeing your **1** in good humour, full of laughter, so you often bring this out in each other with a touch of eccentricity. You can be quick to anger, each of you, but *you* get over it – if **1** lets you. They must do the same, and not brood for too long on an injury.

Accept that you are both ambitious, and try not to outdo each other by wanting to make a grand entrance wherever you go. Pool your resources and make things really happen around you both. Your **1** needs to try to get you to slow down and make time for love. You are both so intolerant of time-wasters and plodding thinkers that you could easily fly to the moon together, but patience is not a strong point for either of you, so you will have to act out of character with each other at times, if you are to grow together and hear what is hurting inside. The possible rewards will be well worth it.

Key themes

Pair of go-getters who neighbours and friends will struggle to keep up with • Hot-tempered flashes between you • Inclined to over-action and exaggeration • Distinctive home with beautiful material furnishings

8 in love with a 2   ★★★★

This is one of the best partnerships in town – especially if the **2** is an **11**. The **2** respects your fairness to others, and your ability (not unlike their own) of seeing both sides of an argument and caring for the underdog. You are good souls in a world of doubters, two people who not only think they can make a difference by being strong and kind to others, but who are *willing to do it*. And your **2** loves your sense of control; your generosity and warmth. Yes – this relationship has serious potential.

8 is a number made up of two circles: a higher and a lower world. What will excite your **2** is the way you can balance a material life with a spiritual and philosophical one. And, just like **2**, **8** is musical, being the number of the octave, with natural rhythm. Your **2** may be more likely to find financial harmony with you than anyone else, and can help you juggle all the requirements of being a good lover, a good citizen, a good business entrepreneur and a good parent. This is a co-operative partnership.

2 loves your honesty, which is usually combined with tact, and which gains even more emphasis from team work with them. They like your appreciation of fine objects, and are willing to build a beautiful home and chic life around you. This is also a very physical bond – one of the best number-partnerships for you to enjoy a strongly sensual, as well as practical, dimension: friends as well as lovers, let's say. 8's humour, style and flamboyance are a foil to 2's subtlety and finesse. When you combine your energies, you tow each other along into more pleasure, more experience. 2 reminds 8, crucially, of the need to stop sometimes and just play, or talk, or rest; and you 're willing to be reminded.

As a couple, you are quite likely to be spiritual (just as with a 7), but, as an 8, you invite your 2 to join in with the highbrow world of successful people – and tactful, gracious

7   6   5   4   3   2   1   9   8

2 will be in their element here. And, it must be said, **2** adds as much to **8**'s brilliant world as anyone can. They are a delicate business ally, a good listener when you have to think out loud, and offer you very good advice, which you willingly heed. This works both ways, and sometimes your **2** will feel you are voicing the very things they were thinking, so well-tuned are your minds.

What works between you works very well. The only thing **2** may have to guard against is a propensity to think a little too well of you: you are, after all, only mortal, and will make mistakes! **8**s see so many options and opportunities, but are sometimes spendthrift and too generous, and **2** can help to counterbalance this with good sense. For some reason, **8** and **2** like to live up high together – whether in a tall block or penthouse, or in a home with a view. Perhaps this is because their lofty thinking really takes flight when they are in the clouds.

Together, **8** and **2** exude a kind of nobility, and offer

| 8 | 9 | 1 | 2 | 3 | 4 | 5 | 6 | 7 |

friends a safe haven in times of stress. **8** often adds professional thought or knowledge to **2**'s exceptional insights, and you will gain a reputation with others for being efficient and fair. **2** reminds **8** of important causes that need help; **8** reminds **2** to be optimistic when the chips are down. Alternately serene together and people-loving, your moods should blend rather than annoy each other, and you will, if anything, enhance each other's individual wisdom with shared observation and conversation. A truly positive opportunity for a happy relationship that should be able to redress momentary lapses of individualism.

Key themes

2 has calming effect on **8** • **8** understands and values **2**'s contributions emotionally and intellectually • Music and material enjoyment important to both, though you are generous to others, too

| 7 | 6 | 5 | 4 | 3 | 2 | 1 | 9 | 8 |

8 in love with a 3   ★★★★★

These numbers work in every possible situation! Whether you met over a drink at work, or on a train going away for a weekend, **8** and **3** are immediately comfortable with one another. You share hope, see the glass half-full instead of half-empty, and have the kind of positivity that makes people around you feel confident trusting in your dreams. Neither of you is so serious that you fail to see the ironies of life – yet you each have a perceptive, generous nature.

What makes an **8** magnetic for a **3** is their far-reaching vision. While **3** looks behind the mask of everyone they meet and, in so doing, breaks down social barriers, you look deep into the soul, and understand others' woes. Bringing these visions together gives you the potential as a pair to be happy in your hearts with one another, but also successful if you work together. You may not have **3**'s

8   9   1   2   3   4   5   6   7

visual agility, and will trust their taste for a final verdict on what looks good decorating a room (or yourself!), but you are creative in ways **3** respects, having a powerful ability to move people with stirring words, which blends nicely with **3**'s wit and charm. And seriously musical **8** makes a cheery tune for **3** to dance through life to.

Sometimes you are so busy looking ahead that you fail to see the pleasures under your nose; **3** helps you correct this oversight. And, when **3** is just too frenetic or buried in the undergrowth to identify a problem or future direction, you cut through the long grass and see the way. **3** has such good ideas and communicative skills, but **8** has the drive and considerable power to make good these concepts. Together, these numbers reach high and low – and everything in between. This leads to some fascinating discoveries and world-changing discussions!

But what **3** loves personally about you is your style, your cachet in the social world, the sense that you have made it to the top from nothing. **3** sees **8**'s vulnerabilities and yet applauds your courage in the face of difficulty; and, while **8** is soul-searching, **3** clowns around and helps you through.

Physically, this is a blending of sensuous energies. **8** is very physical, and **3** likes to create an environment for pleasure, which helps you unwind. **3** reminds you that it is important to have fun in life, and brings you into a social landscape where you will then emphatically win hearts and make a huge impression on others. This is remedial for **8**, for you are apt to encounter tangles in work and responsibility. Also, while **8** is the number of serious money and corporate strength, it has runs of fortune, and may have to start again many times in business. Your **3** has the everyday luck to help you over each bad patch.

But what of high-minded **8**'s attraction to **3**? Why so strong? **3** has levity and yet, beside this, real insight. No one may reduce you to tears of joy more than a **3**. **8** works and struggles, creates a sway in the world and makes an impact; very often, **3** is somewhere there, keeping you going. In a love relationship they can bring affection and joy without being too demanding, because they are sociable enough in a variety of places, and you are not always necessary as the centre of their focus. Potentially dynamic and highly compatible, you supplement each other's skills and desires, and know when to leave each other a little space. After the initial attraction has run its course, real love could well be in the air for you two.

Key themes

3 buoys **8** when **8** is under siege financially or in business • **3** believes in **8**'s real worth • Together, sociable and far-seeing • **3** helps **8** laugh; **8** makes **3** excel in what they do

7   6   5   4   3   2   1   9   8

8 in love with a 4   ★★★

The number **8**, in relationships, is often guilty of taking too much on to itself and overriding the wishes and contributions of a partner. In fact, **8** becomes surprisingly cruel on occasion, when it deems the other person plodding or uninspired. This presents complications for a bond between **4** and **8**, who would otherwise have the utmost respect for each other's code of hard work and achievement in life. This is what would make the two of you excellent companions in the boardroom, but not such a successful pair in the bedroom. You may be too power-hungry, even for a **4**!

4 is naturally attracted to you for your charisma, articulate speech and overall poise, and you both have an honesty and openness that you respect – and function with – together within the relationship. You fill **4** with hope about what may be done with a higher application of the talents you share, and **4** is as much of a doer as you, so there is a real feeling of shared drive and the selection of mutual goals that entices you both. But, perhaps, there is too little romance. If anything, you need a companion who will make you loosen up and relax from time to time – someone who will encourage you to step back and create some inner tranquillity that can help you climb down from the destructive aspects of strain and stress all too common to **8**s. **4** is hardly the number to convince you to sit a dance out! Together you are more likely to lead each other to burn-out.

8 will find **4**'s concerns frankly too banal and solid to suit them for long – for **8** (male or female!) is a tremendous adventurer, the pirate who takes to the high seas. **4** hates such risk, and will want to wag a finger of admonishment when **8** takes a slide – which happens not invariably. **8**s are always building up the material comforts of life, succeeding at business only to find that the wind changes, and they have to start over. This will never suit **4**'s need for security and social conformity. Plus, **8** is perhaps too showy for **4**'s taste, when it's all going well. Expensive clothes and luxuriously decorated houses mesh with your taste for quality rather than quantity – and, to a **4**, this will seem wasteful and irresponsible.

But what *does* work is when the much more expansive vision of the **8** is underscored by the attention to detail brought by **4**. **8** sees everything on the larger scale, but someone adding that ingredient of practicality and method may make this all happen. Again, though, this seems like a relationship where survival and finance can't be separated from the world of lovemaking and emotions. Business may dominate all, and there should be something beyond the achievement of physical and material things. You have a lovely humour, and **4** a loyal heart. Perhaps – with maturity and time – these facets may come to rescue the relationship from the tangle of material concerns.

This pairing rates three stars, though, precisely because of its strengths and its weaknesses. What you see will be what you get – simple as that. Neither number excites the other to those subtle characteristics of creative potential and spiritual or philosophical musings that might come in tandem with other numbers. And **4**'s caution and conservatism seem collision-bound with **8**'s progressive and sweeping manner. A possibly interesting combination, but be realistic about the romance element.

Key themes

All work and not enough play • **8** thinks on a large canvas, **4** perfects the miniature • **8** deems **4** dull at times, and **4** feels **8** is unrealistic • **8** sails the high seas, **4** ties down the sails • Functional material relationship, but business a priority

| 7 | 6 | 5 | 4 | 3 | 2 | 1 | 9 | 8 |

8 in love with a 5   ★★★

When an **8** meets a **5**, other people can see the sparks flying between you. There is a buzz between the two of you,
and it is exciting. You may well have met in the work
arena, where your flamboyant personal styles and sheer
force of character stood out from the grey backdrop
behind you. You are birds of a feather, indeed. Yet you are
also, perhaps, too similar for this to be a wrinkle-free ride.
8 oozes efficiency, and **5** smoulders with potential: it
doesn't take clever **8** more than a moment to see this is
going to be a fascinating encounter.

Your physical attraction may have opened the door,
and it will probably go on working well even when other
facets of your relationship stagger. **5** wants to be reckless
and live wildly, and **8** wants to take control of **5**'s madness
and brilliance. Of course, this could be mutually beneficial,

| 8 | 9 | 1 | 2 | 3 | 4 | 5 | 6 | 7 |

but **5** is not always happy to offer another the control panel, nor are you going to sit back quietly and give them all the limelight for what you both achieve together. Ego clashes seem inevitable. And will it irritate **5** that you try to do all of the jobs and become an icon of industry and achievement?

This is a problem that **8**s also share with **1** lovers: it leaves no time for your personal relationship. Tensions rise and tempers flare when you enter into personal relationships that affect both of you in business (or in business bonds that stray into your personal life). Neither you nor **5** is very good at putting up boundaries, and life may be all work and play mixed together – too high-voltage, not enough quiet time. Burn-out looms, if this is the way you conduct your relationship.

But other facets work well. Both of you have minds that are active, alert, thirsty for knowledge along with the rainfall. With a high degree of sexual energy and adventure,

7 6 5 4 3 2 1 9 8

5 will take you up, up and away: you could really learn to love **5**'s spur-of-the-moment suggestions for out-of-the-way encounters. The one difficulty they will face is to get you home from work and into their passionate embrace. Still, they're good with words, and should work to entice you and begin the seduction process earlier in the day, or even the night before: you'll love your sexy **5** for showing you how to release and unwind.

If you can recognize that you are both risk-takers, and try not to outdo each other – which would definitely lead to ruin! – you might join forces and make things really happen around you both. But there are daily risks – and that's the problem. **8**s can't help attracting attention from admirers and sycophants who long for their power and glamour and vibrancy, and **5**s are simply magnetic to all. Things may spiral out of control, and your **5** will have a job reining in your fierce willpower.

Competitive elements are inevitable, unless you have

reached the wiser platform in your character. Then, it's true, the best shines out: a life of radiance and action, intellectual enquiry and physical effort. Which model are both of you?

Key themes

Lovers who enjoy style, quality and a love of luxury • Comfort and a warm atmosphere suit you both best • Frustrations occur when communication is at cross-purposes or unclear • Competition between you, or bouts of being unrealistic and uncooperative, will sour the relationship

8 in love with a 6   ★★★

With much in common, **6** and **8** are usually close friends.
They work well together, **6** softening some of your over-
ambitious tendencies, enticing you to relax a little. But, as
a love relationship, this is more about physical attraction
and magnetism than ongoing peace. You definitely appreciate **6**'s air of calm, and their wish to keep things running
smoothly; and **6** is impressed with your sheer ability and
capacity to take control in a crisis. But, in personal terms,
you're not always headed in the same direction.

8 sees the world profoundly, sometimes complicating
the picture too much for **6**'s taste; and although you have
distinct quality and professionalism, you can be stubborn
and even faithless when the chips are down – especially in
relationships. **8** always wants to seek solutions to every
enigma, unable to let things rest, whereas **6** needs to take

some things on faith, and tires of the endless delving into thought, politics, personal motivation that fuels your energies. They will definitely be drawn to your air of mystery and authority, but you may at times be just too driven and dissatisfied for peaceable **6**, and certainly you find it difficult to relax if work is demanding. **6** can't fathom this.

6 may, to you, appear over-indulgent with others' foibles, or too complacent about life. It is their way to let things come to them; but, as an **8**, you drive forwards and take charge of fate. While your intelligence and introspection is a source of pleasure and fascination to **6**, they will sometimes feel that your priorities are in the wrong place. There is an unintentionally stern aspect to **8** – are you often too grown-up? – whereas **6** has a Pollyanna outlook on the world, believing that the present is to enjoy.

But what does work between you works well – and the sexual side of the bond may be very good indeed. It is definitely an aphrodisiac for **6** watching you achieve success in difficult situations — and through deep concentration. Loving luxury, they are mesmerized by your control of the material world, delighted by your usual wisdom in discourse with others. **8** is always the wise and fair-minded judge — an attribute that **6** looks up to. Your generosity fits exactly with their spirit, and you will spoil each other with beautiful quality gifts at very opportune moments. And perhaps music will be the greatest bond between you — for **6** alone is almost as musical as **8**, loving the beauty of music. These aspects — drawing each other to higher realms of appreciation — will see the fostering of some very special moments that are personal and binding.

Don't quash your **6**'s enthusiasm for the little things in life; you can be too entrenched in personal difficulties, and forget your sense of humour. And if you have a troubled past, **6** must be very wary: pain may always lurk close to the surface, and only personal achievement may be able to nullify it. **6** simply doesn't want such entanglement.

8	9	1	2	3	4	5	6	7

And why might you love **6**? You are protective, and they need protection, and if you are too serious and over-worked and need hugging **6** is willing to break though your self-imposed asylum. **6** offers much of what you need, including a cocoon in which to ponder while significant ideas form. **8** spends part of its life in darkness, from which amazing seeds can germinate. **6** surrounds you with the kind of serenity and loving security that helps that germination occur. If they love you, they must try to give you solitude sometimes, and demand a little give and take in return. Then, you may do better than your three stars!

Key themes

6 steadies **8** when there is an emergency or crisis • **8** depends on **6**'s genuine admiring love • **6** expands **8**'s creative imagination, and **8** will probably take the lead • Need to respect each other's vulnerabilities

| 7 | 6 | 5 | 4 | 3 | 2 | 1 | 9 | 8 |

8 in love with a 7   ★★★★

8 will entice **7**. Different and yet similar in fascinating ways, the difficulties that a **7** would find in a partnership with another **7** – both loath to balance the material requirements of the world with their own personal priorities – melt away in a partnership with you. You have the ambition **7** often lacks, and yet also offer **7**'s meditative mind some further food for thought.

Anyone involved with an **8** will come to learn that they are doers, power-walkers, thrill-seekers. If something cannot be done in theory, **8** wants to disprove that. Such a viewpoint fascinates **7**, who loves a challenge just from the intellectual standpoint, and, as a pair, you extend each other's vision and sense of possibility. **8** often bluffs through impossible situations, but intelligent **7** shows you a little analytical refinement, and that achievements can

| 8 | 9 | 1 | 2 | 3 | 4 | 5 | 6 | 7 |

still be perfected. This offers a heightened physical attraction and – ultimately – the chance for real love to blossom.

As an **8**, you have much productive fire in your soul, and this may occasionally overwhelm your careful **7**; but you also have what it takes to fire your **7** up – out of intellectual malaise or physical lethargy – into an inspirational mental space. Intelligent **7** has such vision and inner poise, and this in turn challenges you to find a subject worthy of your combined energies – be it in humanitarian enterprises, successful productive business, or in areas of research and academia which forge new understanding and awareness. This can lift **7** into a higher gear, where your mutual adrenaline rush is exciting and stimulating. In other words, **8**'s forceful nature galvanizes **7** into astonishing artistic or intellectual output, and the love develops along the way.

For an **8** – who has a fine mind like **7** – **7** is someone to organize. You see their sensitivity and perceptive powers, and are strongly attracted to that natural hauteur which

7   6   5   4   3   2   1   9   8

sets them apart from the crowd – and you love it. **8**s are only ever excited by quality – never by quantity. Your own cast of mind is philosophical, and looks at both sides of an argument or situation, and your mind will be busy and stocked with varying interests which are guaranteed to intrigue your soul-searching **7**. The good thing is that **7** has the calming personality to make you slow down a little. **8** is a strenuous number, demanding a great deal from the holder, and perhaps only **7** in the wide world has the perceptual power and wisdom to prevent the intriguing, charismatic human being that you are from reaching burn-out. With an **8**, **7** feels needed – though occasionally they will lust for some stillness; **8** is a much more productive number than **7**.

In a nutshell, this is a potential mutual love affair. You must not be too controlling, and must allow **7** to go at its own pace; but you have just the strength your **7** needs to draw on in crisis moments, and **7**'s rationalizing and serene

| 8 | 9 | 1 | 2 | 3 | 4 | 5 | 6 | 7 |

intellectual grasp of all situations can direct your own daring and brilliant mind to the best prize – for both of you.

Key themes

7 channels 8's energies into august projects and inspirational interests · 8 is the strong guide-rail for 7 to hold on to in a downpour · 8 attracts important people, while 7's nobility of character takes both partners to a special plateau of thought and achievement · Strong love

7   6   5   4   3   2   1   9   8

8 in love with an 8   ★★★

Over a breakfast of champagne and smoked salmon with brioche on a not-infrequent basis, you two have a relationship that might be the envy of every mortal being living around you. The attraction is deep – you definitely feel you've known each other before – and the way you communicate is direct and clear but also witty and bantering. No one can see through either of you better than the other. Though you smile through a rainstorm and laugh in heavy winds, another **8** understands that you are putting on a brave face through critical times. And this intrinsic understanding helps, actually: you buffer each other with mutual optimism and determination.

One of the things two **8**s in a relationship feel so attracted to in one other is that, to each of you, nothing – *nothing* – is impossible. Where a **7** asks you to get a reality check when your creative dreams spiral upwards and outwards to untried possibilities, and a **4** thinks you've been indulging in that champagne breakfast too early in the day, another **8** starts the research immediately, to find out what would be involved in the first step of that dream. Nice to be so supported, isn't it?

Difficulties will come if you neglect the romance in the relationship and channel all your energies towards personal successes. You are power meeting power, inspiration meeting strength of will, and a revolution could come from the blending of your combined hopes and talents. This is when sparks literally fly between you, and all around you witness something very special happening. But such drive and singularity of purpose can put a strain on the personal needs each of you have, and you may consequently force each other (albeit unintentionally) towards mental exhaustion and physical/emotional collapse.

When two such characters embrace, there is either a

majestic firework display or the chance that you snuff out each other's brilliance and spark. You are both leaders with grand ideas, and unless you can find a modus operandi where one can support the other at key moments, you may be running powerfully and fast, but in opposite directions. This is why the relationship achieves only three stars.

What brought you into each other's orbit was undoubtedly a shared love for political or cultural thought, musical pleasure and a humorous but tangible appreciation for the Hollywood glamour that life can offer. You also have the philosophical mellowness to know that things are never all good or all bad; there are cycles of comparative wonder and cycles of comparative woe. So, if you listen to the wisdom you've gained individually on one another's behalf, you may offer an outstanding partnership of two kindred souls who can show each other excellence, and strength of character and purpose, quite beyond the reach of any normal pair.

| 8 | 9 | 1 | 2 | 3 | 4 | 5 | 6 | 7 |

As lovers you could really excite each other and fly to the stars of achievement, passion and exploration: two outrageously talented and fearless pirates on the high seas. You could accomplish anything. Just don't let competitiveness or an inability to deliver affection at peak times undermine what could be very good.

Key themes

Good humour and huge enthusiasm for life • Immense energy and inner hope that all will be well • Sometimes neglectful of the need to feed a relationship with outward reassurances of affection (though not cold) • Shared physical stamina • A feeling of knowing each other before

8 in love with a 9   ★★

This is an excellent relationship for two people who want to share much of their life together. **9** is at home with **8**'s good mind and exceptional optimism that everything will come out fine in the end. **8** loves **9**'s genuine good humour and tolerance for all people – though at times you may think your **9** lover a little too undiscerning or forgiving, and that some of their friends aren't worth the investment of time! **8** is definitely more hard-nosed than **9**. But you both have an excellent imagination, and a good attitude towards broader life – recognizing that the world is much bigger than the space which simply surrounds the two of you.

If you are both interested in research or science and factual information (highly likely), you will excite each other and share hours of joy investigating what pleases you. You are both altruistic and have a philanthropic view

8	9	1	2	3	4	5	6	7

of the world and the people around you. Your **9** love is lucky, well-read, and a rounded personality; you have a passion for the spiritual and metaphysical questions about life, and **9** will rove with you into pastures of exploration. Together you may be modernists or medievalists, but you will each be able to make the jump into the other's world.

9 lends you much creative thought and lots of ideas, and you bring to lofty but often unfocused **9** a power and concentration that they may lack. **8** is much more geared to a real and practical life than **9**; but **9** can – and will – teach you to relax and make some personal demands. **8**, in some sense, can be happy and fulfilled by a **9** in a way that may be difficult with other numbers – and this is partly because you are both higher thinkers and somewhat free from social restraints. Both **8** and **9** are spiritual numbers in the most ecumenical sense – neither of you weighted down by tradition or expectation – and, as lovers, this can be very liberating and exciting.

7 6 5 4 3 2 1 9 8

You will love your **9** for their universalist way of thinking. Life is full of surprises with such a soul – a child and yet the most mature person you know. You, equally, gently place **9**'s feet back on the planet when they need grounding – which is not infrequently. A truly enlightened **9** can represent all that is beautiful in the human spirit – musical and artistic, kind and charitable – and this can sometimes make them idealistic, and wishing for perfection. The reality of life can be heartbreaking, and here **8**'s powerhouse character can come to the rescue. You have the magic formula of being able to hold on to one good thing and make it resonate across the bleaker moors of daily struggle, and **9** needs this. Thus, as lovers, you can be like a pair of finely balanced acrobats, creating poetry and fluidity between earth and air.

So why is it, then, that this relationship rates a meagre two stars on the compatibility chart? The answer is that this bond – and it is a powerful one – is a little lacking in romance; not very sensual. If you want a relationship with someone who could be a great friend, someone from whom you will learn and arguably never grow bored with, then it is worth following up the first date. But the danger is that it all may be a little businesslike, and that your sense of fun may not get much exercise. Of course, a friendship/love affair is very grown-up, and has the longevity that passionate flings rarely attain. It ultimately comes down to what you want; but if this love starts, you will go on – at least as lifelong friends – well past the point where most other pairs can run out of steam!

Key themes

May be more about friendship and business than love • Similar mind-sets, and shared interest in a diverse number of cultural and intellectual outlets • 9 calms 8, and 8 puts 9 into a higher gear • Travel may feature strongly

| 7 | 6 | 5 | 4 | 3 | 2 | 1 | 9 | 8 |

8 in love with an 11   ★★★★★

So what does it mean if your **2** partner happens to be a master number **11**? Neither one of you gives up until one of you bursts! A lover born on the 11th or the 29th of the month (as distinct from the pure **2** we looked at earlier) will excite your interest because they have so much light and inner intensity. For you, you recognize that your **11** lover is an inspiration to others and carries a sense of the divine mission – whether they are a scientist, a sceptic or a spiritual seeker.

You love this person's style and personal magnetism, their hunger for a life that is deeply lived. What is so sexy about your **11** love is their vivid response to all that exists – to the scent of a flower, or the sound of a heartbeat. You, too, have moments when this intensity seems normal. An **11** sets your mind whirring with all that may be built by a fired dreamer and a diligent architect of dreams.

Wrinkles occur in the silk taffeta when your fascinating **11** becomes egocentric – and this does happen, at times – but you have enough sanity and stubborn strength to anchor them back down in reality, making them take themselves a little less seriously when required, and forbidding them to believe so completely in their own publicity. When your **11** has an attack of ego, you will remedy the ill. They can get away with little around you, for you see and understand all. This is more likely to have a positive than a nullifying effect.

And the spiritual light in **11**'s eyes rests on you because they love the ground others give you, the way you face down dull opposition from flabby minds. An **11** is image-conscious, and they like the way you can work this – making an entrance to your own advantage, drawing others to eat from your hand. Your charisma and dynamism is tangible ... but markedly different to theirs. And this works as a good difference — even a romantic one. You lead each other on into new worlds.

Don't shrink from telling this physically and spiritually shining person when they are being unintentionally unkind or outrageous beyond good manners. You have both the strength and vision to stand up to them on occasion, which is excellent; 11's only real adversary is themselves, and your love affair will blossom all the more over time if they know they can trust you to tell them when things are getting out of hand. Neither of you can stomach plodding people or a culturally and intellectually bereft world, but there are ways of fighting this, and a head-on collision with others is not that way. This, you know — but **11** may not!

It is truly an exhilarating flight, this partnership, and you will enjoy a head-in-the-clouds feeling often.

Key themes

Shared sense of daring and exceptional possibility about life · **8** stands up to **11**'s ego, but also evens out their energy with practicality · Magnetic physical attraction and similar thrust towards a colour-enriched life

8 in love with a 22   ★★★★

Is your **4** partner also a master number **22**? As with master number **11**, a love born on the 22nd of the month also offers you a powerful and uplifting tie. You recognize from the first glimpse someone who seems masterly in every way – a cut above the average; and, in truth, you are always pulled to someone who stands out in the crowd, for **8** cannot love a completely mortal being, looking for a touch of the god or goddess in anyone you give your heart to. Well, here is another such one. Like an **11**, a **22** has a light and a radiance of being – albeit on a slightly more practical and material body. **22** can withstand the pressures of a real life, and this is something you will appreciate.

Now, then, your **22** lover is diplomatic and has more understanding of the ordinary world than **11** – who is

| 8 | 9 | 1 | 2 | 3 | 4 | 5 | 6 | 7 |

always surprised to find that the rest of the world doesn't dream like they do! – but there is still an issue of ego. **22** won't brook idiotic ideas or foolish thoughts, and anyone who subscribes to the banal is less than visible to them. At times you may need to tell them when it is sensible to be pragmatic, but at least **22** can spell 'pragmatism', whereas your **11** prospective lover never can – and this is what makes a **22** master-number relationship more amenable, more workable ... and also a tad less thrilling! Maybe this is because your **22** love is a little less of a challenge than that perfect, five-star **11** relationship.

You two would generate a lot of business together – and, in fact, it is likely that you first spotted each other in a business environment, because you would unquestionably shine out in the crowd for each other. You would have noticed at once that your classically elegant **22** could handle everyone with the same efficiency as you, and that they exuded an instinctive control over other people in the room. This is an aphrodisiac for you, making you want to know them more, to talk to them more, from that first sighting. And this is mutual, for the **22** understands something of your complexity even after just a brief conversation, and this, for them, is a honeycomb for a bee to fly to, rather than a deep well to be avoided.

And, always proud of the person you step out with being in a league of their own, you love that this interesting person looks as if their clothes were hand-tailored for them, and that their style is both careful and quietly dazzling. An **11** will shimmer in public for you (even the men!), while a **7** will exude polish and grace to make you proud, but a **22** casts a gentle bewitchment with their physical appearance, which, at close quarters, no one can exactly explain. It's inherent, perhaps, and you love it. Get through the first holiday together, and this partnership could go on and on ...!

| 8 | 9 | 1 | 2 | 3 | 4 | 5 | 6 | 7 |

Key themes

Both confident and stand-out people whom others look to
· Mutual pride in each other adds a dimension of sexiness
and respect · Happiness comes down to having enough
time to cement the bond at the beginning of the
relationship

Work

YOUR **WORK** COMPATIBILITY CHART

	1	2	3	4	5
With a 1	★★★★	★★★★★	★	★★★	★★
With a 2	★★★★★	★★★	★★★	★★★★	★
With a 3	★	★★★	★★★★	★★	★★★★
With a 4	★★★	★★★★	★★	★★★★★	★★★
With a 5	★★★	★	★★★★★	★★★	★★
With a 6	★★	★★★★★	★★★★	★★★★	★★★
With a 7	★★★★★	★★★	★★★	★★★★★	★★
With an 8	★★★★★	★★★★★	★★★★★	★★★	★★★
With a 9	★★★★	★★★	★★★★★	★★	★★★
With an 11	★★	★★★★	★★★	★★★★★	★★
With a 22	★★★★★	★★	★★★	★★★	★★★

6	7	8	9	11	22
★★	★★★★★	★★★★★	★★★★	★★	★★★★★
★★★★	★★★	★★★★★	★★★	★★★★	★★
★★★★	★★★	★★★★★	★★★★★	★★★	★★★
★★★★	★★★★★	★★★	★★	★★★★★	★★★
★★★★	★★	★★★★	★★★	★★	★★★★
★★★	★	★★★★	★★★	★★★★★	★★★★
★	★★★★	★★★	★★	★★★★	★★★★★
★★★★	★★★	★★★	★★★★	★★★★★	★★★★
★★★	★★	★★★★	★★★	★★★★★	★★★★★
★★★★	★★★★	★★★★★	★★★★★	★★★★	★★★★★
★★★★	★★★★★	★★★★	★★★★★	★★★★★	★★★

7	6	5	4	3	2	1	9	8

8 working with a 1   ★★★★★

The very idea of this pairing spells 'big business'. Here are a couple of potential moguls, and if you are both languishing in a corner doing unspectacular things you are under-selling your capabilities and under-achieving. Perhaps no one has more natural talent for business than you two, but you need distinct roles to avoid a strong clash of wills!

If you're looking for an inspired partner to form a business with, look no further. You think on the grand scale, which **1** will love – for no obstacles are really an impediment to success for the two of you. Just like you, **1** likes to have more than one project on the go, and if you are given charge of a business which is failing, or limping along, the two of you can move it to unsuspected heights. **8** never relies on luck, but finds out exactly what is needed and provides it. Usually well-educated (even if self-taught), your

8	9	1	2	3	4	5	6	7

mind is ready to see potential in what the **1** is imagining, and to help **1** get their concept out there. If a new project of **1**'s design requires a crash course in some new field, or a mastery of any previously untried discipline, you will find the means to do it. No one can see **1**'s visions as clearly, or understand better how to set **1** ticking until you find a way to change the existing landscape. You appreciate **1**'s spark.

Emergency situations will somehow frequently arise around the two of you – because you push each other, and everyone else, to the top of their game. Be warned not to run yourselves ragged in pursuit of perfection, and allow each other the freedom of your own patch, so you don't thwart one another's intentions.

Key themes

Excellent for sparking off each other • Complementary skills • Generate humour and largesse with colleagues

| 7 | 6 | 5 | 4 | 3 | 2 | 1 | 9 | 8 |

8 working with a 2   ★★★★★

An excellent inner communication and effortless feeling of harmony that affects all is produced here. You share the same instincts for what works, what pleases, and how to get others on board. There is, simply, a rapport between you.

There is always a feeling of expectation around **2** and **8**. Perhaps there is a frisson of attraction which sets up the added dynamic; or, it could be the way one understands the other without redundant explanation. It is so good that it would make an excellent business partnership where you each work for yourselves. **8** has the dream of higher remuneration, and **2** backs this up with earthy suggestions **8** respects. **2** humours **8** when necessary, and makes a lighter atmosphere, which is good for everyday tranquillity. Best of all, **2** pre-empts **8**'s needs, and knows before you do what will be required in a project that may only be in its

| 8 | 9 | 1 | 2 | 3 | 4 | 5 | 6 | 7 |

planning phase, astonishing you by producing facts at the appropriate moment like so many rabbits from hats.

Even when emergency situations arise – which they will, as **2** pushes your ability to the wire – you have a knack together of resolving any crisis before it becomes too threatening. **2** diffuses the tension, and helps you maintain the steely control and determination for which **8**s are justly famous. And, if you seem to be the dynamo, don't imagine **2**'s vital role as anchor, bantering charmer and organized thinker is overlooked by anyone – least of all by you, who will sing their praises even when they have no way of knowing, This is potentially a truly excellent work relationship waiting to take off.

Key themes

Inspire each other's strengths • Work with humour and instinct • Balance each other's needs • Frisson of attraction?

7 6 5 4 3 2 1 9 8

8 working with a 3   ★★★★★

A shared purpose brings you two together for a really first-rate business bond. **8** understands how **3** thinks and why they do what they do – you really appreciate their tact and style. They can charm any reluctant client or third party into agreement with what you want – at any price, it seems – and you use your people skills as the jumping-off point for your own designs in business. No one has a better head for what has real potential than an **8**, and **3** gives everything to help you achieve the desired end result.

8 trusts **3** to come up with those appealing little twists and necessary variations on a theme which make for a more harmonious work environment. Knowing **3** has the humour to cope with any emergency, you may ask them to take on a pressure situation, where other numbers fail to see that **3** has what it takes. You are completely at

8	9	1	2	3	4	5	6	7

ease with **3**'s facile mind, good memory and witty way of deflecting criticism or crisis. In short, nobody gives **3** more leeway to shine, or more benefit of the doubt about imaginative propositions. **8** takes **3** very seriously.

And who else besides a **3** recognizes the intentions of **8**'s brilliance? Others may think you are being too clever for the world, but if there is any way of popularizing your genius, **3** will find that way. And, together, you will bring a whirr of activity and a sense of pride in achievement to everyone working with you. **3** nurses **8** through many sleepless nights – to a sunny new day!

Key themes

Bounce off one another's energies and visions • **3** recognizes **8**'s professionalism, and **8** happily gives **3** opportunity • Very good prospects for success

8 working with a 4   ★★★

Though this pairing rates three stars, the truth will be either considerably worse than this or markedly better. If the **4** is solid and reliable, with a penchant for accountancy skills and hours of hard work, you will respect them for this, though will feel obliged to take the lead in matters of policy and public profile. But if the **4** is more old-fashioned, and doesn't take chances, you'll look on them with impatience.

8 combines **4**'s work talents and drive with **1**'s ability to see what the market will want in five years' time, and this is sometimes too much for **4**. Like **1** and **5**, **8** is an innovator and philosopher – and the blend of quasi-divine inspiration you receive, along with the real desire to make the world sit up and take notice, is not **4**'s favourite way of doing things. They may come to resent your arrogance (as they see it), and your wish to be too much in control.

8	9	1	2	3	4	5	6	7

What works well is that you will rely on **4**'s discretion, honesty and hard work to back up your lead and follow through on ideas. You give **4** true praise for the kind of resourcefulness and tenacity that perhaps only an **8** really observes. Many people take a **4**'s persistence for granted – even tease them about it; **8**, on the contrary, recognizes that, without such grind, talent is only half of a business. And **4** will give you your due, understanding your enviable degree of will and personal strength that is a beacon for others. The real test will come on day one. If you can survive your first week working together, and get over the clashes of method, perhaps you are both en route to building an empire.

Key themes

Division of power important • If **8** not too high-handed and impatient, **4** is the model employee

| 7 | 6 | 5 | 4 | 3 | 2 | 1 | 9 | 8 |

8 working with a 5   ★★★★

Here are a couple of potential workaholics; if you haven't taken off yet, you are both failing in your capabilities. **5** and **8** hold similarities: both of you are venturesome, progressive, resourceful, skilful, straightforward, capable and courageous. **8** never, though (unlike **5**), trusts to luck, but finds out exactly what is needed and provides it.

Your mind is ready to see potential in **5**'s dreams, and you know just how to actualize their business ideas. As with a **1**, if a new project of **5**'s design requires a crash course or learning to master a previously untried discipline, **8** will do it. No one can see how **5**'s brilliant mind is working better than you, but you also know how to light the touch paper under a **5**, and get them moving in a more focused direction. You have a humour for **5**'s madness, but take their occasional genius very seriously. And, as **8**s are

8	9	1	2	3	4	5	6	7

excellent managers with a disciplined financial awareness, you support and pre-empt **5**'s practical needs (and will have appointed an office manager to handle the practicalities).

You will often need to fly by the seats of your pants, as they say: **5**s need to be reminded about sequential process and responsibility to complete what they have undertaken, but fortunately **8** has 'big business' stamped on its forehead, and you expect results from **5**. **5** can't fool you, and probably won't let you down – rising to greater heights than ever under your tutelage. Be warned not to run yourselves ragged by over-reaching, or over-estimating your worth, and allow each other the freedom of your own patch, so you don't thwart one another's intentions.

Key themes
Complementary skills • **8** provides stability for **5**, and **5** responds to the goals **8** sets out for them

| 7 | 6 | 5 | 4 | 3 | 2 | 1 | 9 | 8 |

8 working with a 6   ★★★★

In truth, **8** – the number of business and money matters – works well with most people, so it is no surprise to see a solid tie between two amiable souls. **6** will have to exercise a little patience now and again, because you dance to a different drum to most people and are, well, driven! Sometimes there are other things to do besides work. But **6** will definitely get ample opportunity with an **8** to show what they're made of. You will really value their more aesthetic and decorative contributions to basic business ventures – whether this means the dressing-up of a product or the flourishes that strengthen bonds with other businesspeople. You can trust **6** to add a certain polish and finesse.

And **6** enjoys having someone inspiring to be imaginative for. **8** is a number which never doubts any possibility, and this extraordinary dynamism combined with an inclination to dig to find research and resources will empower the sometimes docile **6**, who is dying to show what they can really do, but lacking confidence about it. **6** will bask in **8**'s assurances of interest and commitment; you give them confidence, and they blossom for it.

8s always have a goal – unless you temporarily lose your way through over-extending yourself – and **6** can play a vital calming role in an **8**'s business life. Also, **8** already has strong commercial tendencies and an appreciation of the luxury market, and **6** will add a desirable feeling of harmony to the work environment. Overall, this is a powerful tie with a great chance for financial and personal success, allowing **6** to find their true brilliance in their best field.

Key themes

6 softens **8**'s fervency in a positive way • **8** takes the lead and brings dynamism • **6** packages **8**'s exhilarating ideas

8 working with a 7   ★★★

Though these two numbers spark off each other very well in a personal relationship, they are – surprisingly – not so well suited in business. Such different methods are attractive in a personal bond, but in the boardroom 7 is frightened at times by 8's approach, and 8 is disappointed at clever 7's lack of acumen about money. Not that 7 is foolish around finances, but 8 will always need a reliable, up-front partner who is as courageous and flamboyant as they are. You see endless possibilities, while 7 is not so driven by the material world. Day to day, as friends or lovers, this isn't a problem: in fact, 8's attention to financial requirements gives 7 the freedom not to be so fettered. But, in a work relationship, this becomes a frustration for both of you.

From the practical, material point of view, an 8 realizes only too well that pragmatism is often necessary in the world of financial reality. Although **7** has finesse and vision, they are unwilling to bend over backwards for anyone they see as dishonest or unscrupulous. **8** can bite their tongue, but **7** cannot. And so **7**'s famous honesty becomes a thorn in your side ... which is not to say that **7**'s moral feelings are not absolutely justified; but you see the need to be a diplomat, to flatter and cajole, whereas this is below **7**'s dignity.

In working life, other people will love or loathe, lionize or lose it with a **7** for their pride and hauteur. An **8** – remaining dignified but flexible – will tear their hair out. So, not impossible, but definitely a high-wire act where both of you must do a lot of balancing!

Key themes

8 may seem too carnivorous about business for herbivorous **7** • Excellent minds which need room to function

7   6   5   4   3   2   1   9   8

8 working with an 8   ★★★

Wouldn't you think this would be perfection in the board-room? Surely, together, this is a Rothschild dynasty about to unfold? And so, occasionally, it may prove ...

Truthfully, however, two **8**s working in tandem tend to snuff out each other's fire. You may be guilty, in unison, of over-action on various strands of work – of pushing just too hard to attain a result without thinking of what is in your mutual interests. There is little 'softly-softly' approach – and at times this is required. If you bring out the negative sides of your characters, you will find yourselves becoming impatient with others or getting lost behind the desire for too much outward extravagance and display. Someone needs to balance your fierce energy and will, and make sure that your extraordinarily strenuous drive is to the best purpose – otherwise, **8** can have blind spots like everyone

| 8 | 9 | 1 | 2 | 3 | 4 | 5 | 6 | 7 |

else, and fail to see when a project should be sidelined. Then, burn-out is certain, and money difficulties must come, too.

Yet the rating of three stars is not given lightly, and if you can find a way to allocate different departments to one another, so that you are working in sync rather than in competition, you may take any business to a higher level. Two **8**s have double the need to work on the grand scale, not to be fenced in by lack of opportunity or too few interests on the horizon. **8** is always developing in business, and if the field is too small nothing good will come of it. Give each other room to breathe, and understand that what you don't like in each other is what you don't like in yourself. It could be a lesson – and still be a material success!

Key themes

Not always in sync, but when you are there is judgement and extraordinary stamina • Danger of being competitive

7 6 5 4 3 2 1 9 8

8 working with a 9   ★★★★

9s possess an excellent imagination and a strong vision: you can harness that vision and paint something masterly. With a flair for the dramatic and the absurd, **9** can recover some of **8**'s playfulness, and bring a wonderful balance between success and pleasure into the work arena.

You are both showmen, with a feeling for the spectacular, paying detailed attention to the impact everything may have on a client or in the marketplace. **9** has an essential talent in many creative fields, but not always the best organizational skills or understanding of their own clever ideas. As an **8**, you remedy this pretty smartish, showing the often distracted **9** how to assemble such a plethora of gifts into a manageable and desirable package or product.

Whatever business you happen to work in – and best if it is in either a creative or a political landscape – think of

| 8 | 9 | 1 | 2 | 3 | 4 | 5 | 6 | 7 |

the marriage of **8** and **9** in business as the entrepreneur (**8**) seeing the opportunities around the performer/actor (**9**). This will apply even if your vocational domain is in science or medicine. **8** must direct and manage **9**'s talent; and if **9** drops into a moody state or becomes depressed (as often happens), who do you suppose can chivvy them out of it? **8** has the power like no other number to achieve constructive material accomplishments which also have an altruistic or socially responsible edge, and **9** will blossom under such tutelage. **8** is often a force to be seen to be believed, but you can become a slave to your intellect sometimes. **9** can help you recover some much-needed feeling, and together you could discover pleasure and prosperity.

Key themes

Profitable curiosity, with different ways of seeing • Blend of feeling, courage and sense • Makes good business

| 7 | 6 | 5 | 4 | 3 | 2 | 1 | 9 | 8 |

8 working with an 11   ★★★★★

What is good and progressive with a **2** reaches even a shade higher with this master-number bond. Adding **8** and **11** we come to '19', which gives us **1** – thinking as one unit. But in the tarot, '19' is also the card called 'The Sun' – and radiance is what you may achieve here.

If the **11** is reasonably focused on material success, it will be their perseverance and intelligence blended with a good imagination that brings them out on top. And this can just as easily describe a positive and well-directed **8** – so you see how this results in 'thinking as one'. You could come together to create real abundance in your lives – especially if you are working in your own linked business.

Your own leadership talents may see you move into the public arena – either in performance or in the public service – when you meet and work with an inspired **11**. You

8	9	1	2	3	4	5	6	7

are both expressive, and if you have the courage to challenge the **11** on some points (which most would hesitate to do) you may lecture large groups or the wider community with a powerful and illuminating result. **11** and **8** together will attract both admiration and money, but you will also remember your responsibility to make a difference somewhere. **11** motivates and inspires you – a task you normally fulfil for others. This amounts to a mutual respect and esteem ... not that there won't be clashes of temperament and contrasting views. But **8** fills in some of the technique **11** is missing, and gets them back on the rails when they are simply flying too fast and too dangerously. And what a shining palace you should enjoy together ...

Key themes

Tremendous vitality and intellect • Able to overcome many obstacles and design wonderful business ideas

| 7 | 6 | 5 | 4 | 3 | 2 | 1 | 9 | 8 |

8 working with a 22   ★★★★

A **22** will be as focused and aware as you of the value of spinning straw into gold, and **22** has a nose, like you, for how to achieve this. As long as your concepts are practical and well-organized, you will manage to think in the most sweeping terms and yet on the most concentrated canvas.

A **22** always has the potential to accrue wealth and fame, yet they feel that personal enlightenment is also important. This amounts to a social conscience which benefits, to a greater or smaller extent, from whatever they do in business, and your own genius for thinking in fairly broad terms while recognizing the need for the practical will work very well with theirs. You each have fairly strong characters, but when directed towards practical business directives this can be an exceptionally successful partnership.

Ideally, a **22** working with an **8** would seek ways to use

8   9   1   2   3   4   5   6   7

a healthy business return to improve the world around you both. Sponsoring sports and public health awareness, or backing fledglings in business, or designing books and television slots that have an uplifting and educative purpose, are aspects of work that appeal to no one more than you two. So, why not the perfect five stars? That three-letter word beginning with 'e' is still a problem here: you are each egocentric about business, used to not being challenged, to not having to explain yourselves to lower workers on the food chain. It will be the brass section of the orchestra warming up, when you are asked to face each other, but such a challenge may be very good for both of you.

Key themes

22 likes to be 'master' with a willing apprentice, but will soon discover this is not the way forward with an **8** • Mutual originality sparks wonderful solutions to problems

7	6	5	4	3	2	1	9	8

Friendship

YOUR **FRIENDSHIP** COMPATIBILITY CHА

	1	2	3	4	5
With a 1	★★★	★★★★★	★★	★★★	★★★
With a 2	★★★★★	★★	★★★	★★★★	★
With a 3	★★	★★★	★★★★	★	★★★
With a 4	★★★	★★★★	★	★★★★★	★★
With a 5	★★★	★	★★★★	★★	★★★
With a 6	★	★★★★	★★★★★	★★★	★★★
With a 7	★★★★	★★★★★	★★★★	★★★★★	★
With an 8	★★★★	★★★★★	★★★★★	★★	★★★
With a 9	★★★★	★★★	★★★★	★★★★	★★★
With an 11	★★★	★★★★★	★★	★★★★★	★★
With a 22	★★★	★★★	★★★★	★★	★★★

8 9 1 2 3 4 5 6 7

6	7	8	9	11	22
★	★★★★	★★★★	★★★★	★★★	★★★
★★★	★★★★★	★★★★	★★★	★★★★★	★★★
★★★★	★★★★	★★★★★	★★★★	★★	★★★★
★★★	★★★★★	★★	★★★★	★★★★★	★★
★★★	★	★★★★	★★★★	★★	★★★
★★★	★	★★★★	★★★★	★★★	★★★★★
★	★★★★	★★★	★★	★★★★★	★★★★★
★★★★	★★★	★★★★	★★★★	★★★★★	★★★
★★★★	★★	★★★★	★★	★★★★	★★★★
★★★	★★★★★	★★★★★	★★★★	★★★★★	★★★★
★★★★	★★★★★	★★★	★★★★	★★★★	★★

7   6   5   4   3   2   1   9   8

Interested in an extraordinary range of people, you make lasting friendships with many famous or unusual souls. Let's see which are the best combinations ... and which are the worst:

8 and **1** (★★★★): This is good, though **1**'s 'I am' ego wrong-foots many; **8** is not cowed by **1**'s occasional lack of finesse or apology for wanting to get on with things. You are in the same groove, and you are strong enough not to take offence at **1**'s brutal honesty. You dish it out, too!

8 and **2** (★★★★): A very strong friendship for different reasons. **2** soothes and sweet-talks you out of the growing headache when everyone else seems so slow-witted or guarded. And you will look after a **2**, and be surprised when the favour is returned with more strength and sense than you expected.

8 and **3** (★★★★★): Good company for each other. **3** loves your magnitude and makes you laugh out loud; you may race each other to pick up the bill, but when you are going through a bad patch only **3** has the implicit spirit to see you over it. An almost romantic friendship.

8 and **4** (★★): You may feel slowed up a little by **4**. You respect and foster this careful thinker and diligent soul, enjoying much about their honesty and purpose. But it is a different mind-set you enter into, and when you really want to run and leap **4** might be lead-footed. **4** draws in sepia, while you think in technicolour. Good, honest, but limited.

8 and **5** (★★★★): You generate understanding instantly. **5** is one of those numbers others love or hate, but you just get their vivacity and energy, and see it to a better purpose. It is their imagination you warm to, and together you are up for anything socially. You learn from each other.

7 6 5 4 3 2 1 9 8

8 and **6** (★★★★): You are drawn to **6**'s gentle magnetism, and their softness. If you always live in the fast lane, you will arrive at a roadside lay-by out of petrol. **6** rescues, calms, and allows you to feel you can slow down just occasionally. You share good taste, and are good co-hosts.

8 and **7** (★★★): This works more or less, because **8** – seeing two sides of all situations – finds a point of contact with everyone. It is **7**'s cerebral existence that maddens you. You love their precise analysis, their reticence and style; but they are too admonitory even for you at times. You'll love them, or they will send you wild with frustration!

8 and **8** (★★★★): This friendship may send you both bust! **8** is not cautious financially anyhow, and another **8** may drive you to the edge of reason. But, on the plus side, you will have such an experience of life – of travel and conversation and luxurious living. Does it matter if you go wild?

8   9   1   2   3   4   5   6   7

8 and **9** (★★★★): You recognize intelligence and the ability to think deeply in each other. **9** entertains you, makes you see the silly side of life, and is an excellent drinking or dancing companion when you need one. You are higher souls. Moody, at times, too.

8 and **11** (★★★★★): Business and love relationships between you work well, so why wouldn't friendship, too? The two of you emit something cheeky and yet spiritual to the world – as though you both share a secret we should all know. If we could only reach it!

8 and **22** (★★★): When the material or romantic world draws you two together, sparks fly. Literally. Sometimes you seem way above the banal together; sometimes you can turn the banal into something edifying and entertaining. You will love **22**'s style and interest in quirky things, while they will find you full of surprises. Strong friends.

8 IN OTHER PLACES

So what does it mean when your number turns up on a house? Do you live in an 8 home? And how does the number 8 affect your pet – or even the car that you drive? Numbers exude a subtle influence on everything in our lives; and here are just a few examples of how ...

8 9 1 2 3 4 5 6 7

An 8 address

If the number of your address – or of your apartment – reduces back to an **8**, you have an address of distinction. It is impossible for it not to exude a sense of class, luxury or glamour; and it is unlikely that – for the length of the street – there is any house more probable to repay the investment that is put into it. An **8** house makes money.

If you are living here, you already show signs of focus and achievement; the house was built for someone who would achieve independence and self-mastery. Living in an **8** home you will need to be aware of the needs of neighbours on both sides – seeing two sides of every situation – but if you have a well-defined goal in life, and an understanding of how to deal with people, you will bring this to bear on all relationships with property. In an **8** home, work comes back with you. Use good judgement in who comes to share it or add design elements to it.

7   6   5   4   3   2   1   9   **8**

An 8 pet

If you don't know your pet's birthday, use the first letter of their name to calculate their number. If it's an H, Q or Z, they're an **8**. An **8** dog is a big dog with a gentle nature who knows its own strength very well and doesn't have the need to bark other than occasionally. Stretched out in front of the fire in a large home, it will seem to exemplify all that is noble, generous and openly friendly about the house and its owners. And this, if you like, is the way to describe an **8** pet – whether it's a dog, a guinea pig or a Shetland pony. This pet knows it is something a little bit special, and handles visitors with dignity and personal pride.

Even if your pet is a tiny puppy not much bigger than a teacup pooch, it just knows life is meant to be luxurious and good. It will spoil both partners in a relationship with its attentions, never stuck on one person alone; and, if it's a cat, it will want the most comfortable bed to lie on – but will work for its keep, too, keeping down mice or asking anyone knocking on the door to think twice if they have mischievous intentions. An **8** pet of any kind will protect you and dream deep, philosophical dreams in the firelight.

An 8 car

If the numbers of your licence plate reduce to **8**, this car tells you you've made it. Even if it's only a Mini Cooper or a Fiat Cinquecento, it will still – somehow – have the heart of a Rolls Royce or a Cadillac. Perhaps they only give out **8** licence plates to such cars? It may be the first car you buy with your own money, or a present from a well-heeled admirer, or even a 'self-congratulation' for a promotion. An **8** car says quality, not quantity. You could have bought a four-wheel drive but chose something smaller that you could afford which still said 'dignified taste'. But, it may cost some money over time. And it's worth every penny.

7   6   5   4   3   2   1   9   **8**

YOUR LIFE NUMBER
Your lesson to learn

The time has come to consider the other main number in your numerology chart: your Life Lesson, or LIFE, number. This is sometimes also called the 'Birth Force'. Just as for the DAY number, calculating your LIFE number is easy: simply add together each digit of your full birth date (day, month and year), and keep adding the digits until they reduce to a single number (*see example on page 270*).

And that's it. You have your Life number.
So what does it tell us?

| 8 | 9 | 1 | 2 | 3 | 4 | 5 | 6 | 7 |

What does it mean?

The **LIFE** number takes times to show its mark. You should see its influence over many years, and understand that it is representative of certain strengths and weaknesses that we learn to live with through years of experience. These characteristics need to be analysed over time, and it can take a while for us to come to know ourselves truly from our **LIFE** number. Uncovering these aspects of our character is a process of discovery, and we often don't fully recognize the traits of this number as clearly, or as quickly, as those of the stronger **DAY** number.

Once you have done your sums and discovered this second important number, you'll want to find out what this means. If your **LIFE** and **DAY** numbers are the same, this powerfully reinforces the qualities of your own number, and accentuates both strengths and weaknesses. You won't be fighting corners within your personality by having

7 6 5 4 3 2 1 9 8

two numbers to live with that are, perhaps, miles apart in spirit. But then, equally, if your numbers are the same you may lack a broad vision of the world, seeing with very sharp eyes through just a single (though enormous!) window.

On the following pages we will examine what your **DAY** number 8 is like in tandem with each other number, beginning with the powerful doubling of **8 DAY** and **8 LIFE**, and then moving on through all other possible combinations. If you discover you have a **LIFE** number which totals **11** or **22**, before it reduces to a final single digit of **2** or **4**, read the entry for **8** and **2**, or **8** and **4**, but also pay special attention to any extra information given relating to the added significance of the number being a variation of a master number.

SAME **DAY** AND **LIFE** NUMBER

With **8** as both your DAY and your LIFE number, you are on a mission! Your powers of organization should be exemplary. You will be quite an independent thinker with an individual and forceful personality, and your energy and feeling for the life force is likely to be considerable. Throughout your life anything can – and will – happen, and you are usually capable of taking charge of any event or circumstance and foraging a path through the most tangled woods ... and you may have to. Never forget who you are or what you can do if you put your mind to it.

On with the show

These numbers linked together make you a combination of the showman and the philosopher, with a pinch of mysticism that is natural and not forced in any way. A cocktail of John Lennon and Mata Hari blended with, perhaps, Harry Houdini – this last, because **8**s have escapes from all kinds of difficult tests throughout the many years of their emotional relationships and business adventures, and a double **8** seems able to twist into amazing shapes, just like the digit itself, to mould to any new position.

Only the figures of '**8**' and '**0**' have the capacity to make an endless motion without retreating or stopping and starting again – a perpetual cycle of motion. Thus, as a double **8**, you keep moving under the most extraordinary circumstances.

8   9   1   2   3   4   5   6   7

Something in the heir?

If your **LIFE** number totalled '35' in your addition, before reducing to **8**, you have the number of inheritance, and it is likely that you will either inherit money or power – or both – at some time in your life. In any case, double **8** – whatever actual total you reach for the **LIFE** number – does indeed often bring a significant windfall in the shape of inheritance or a strange connection with fate, for **8** is the number of karma (the law of return), and in some way you are receiving throughout your life some response to what you have given to others. A double **8** will also make the most gifted speaker, teacher or executive. These numbers also suggest that what you do will be on your own merits – though luck comes eventually, too.

Don't worry if you meet some serious opposition at various times in your life. Like a born lawyer – or, even more, a high court judge! – you have the powers of speech

7   6   5   4   3   2   1   9   8

that can turn straw into gold and charm unicorns to your door. There is no need for you to go without, no reason for you to be unhappy. Your friendliness and personal charm should make you attractive to both sexes and to all classes of people, and achieving emotional balance and joy will be a priority.

It's likely that you will probably feel a faith in spiritual or philosophical truths and laws, too, and you are very capable of mastering the most difficult problems. Dig deep when you need to, for you will rarely come off second best if you have the mind to emerge in sunlight.

Double trouble?

If your **DAY** number **8** is coupled with a **LIFE** number totalling (before it reduces to **8**) '44' – the master variant of **8** – more is demanded of you in your life. You need to discover your own self-discipline and realize that you have

8   9   1   2   3   4   5   6   7

a serious mission: to achieve material goals and use some part of your profit for the good of others.

With '44' in the equation you will feel more than a tinge of irritation with people who don't quickly understand what you're telling them. Mortals, beware! You may also be very strong physically indeed, even if you're quite little! Every variant of double **8** tells a tale of someone with guts and humour, of the potential talent to show all of us old dogs many new tricks. A double **8** jumps on no one's bandwagon: quite simply, they set new standards in everything.

Friends forever

You will keep your friends your life long. Be ready to book a large venue for your big 'zero' birthdays, because it will be impossible to draw the line at who you want to be there. You have excellent powers of discrimination, but you get on with an array of folk from every country under the sun (and a few in the extreme cold, too!). Your talent is to get Bill Clinton chatting comfortably with Marilyn Manson while you keep the local vicar intrigued on some unlikely and unusual subject about Mexican festivals of the dead. It's all the same to a double **8**!

DIFFERENT **DAY** AND **LIFE** NUMBERS

Most of us will find that we have two different birthday numbers, and this can be an advantage. One number may soften the single track of the other, and mean we can see other people's viewpoints more easily. At other times, though, the numbers may be in real conflict – and this leads to vacillation in our reactions to everyday situations, or confusion about why we want to run one way and then another.

In the following pages you will discover how your own two numbers are likely to work together, and what you can do to maximize the potential of both when they are paired up.

7   6   5   4   3   2   1   9   8

8 Day with 1 Life

Who will succeed at business in this world if you don't? These two numbers understand that, while money isn't everything, without it life is harder. You will almost certainly work for yourself, or independently, and you will work very hard in fits and starts. In fact, you work hard and play hard, and can have extraordinary bursts of physical energy when you need it ... which translates as: watch the inclination to push yourself too hard, at times! And in this life that often seesaws between work and play, family and finance, don't be surprised if you make and lose, and then remake, many fortunes or successful lines of expression. Each of these two numbers can be prone to win, lose and win again, but with both together this kind of oscillation seems unavoidable. Perhaps it is really your way of putting yourself through perpetual challenges?

| 8 | 9 | 1 | 2 | 3 | 4 | 5 | 6 | 7 |

So bold are your two numbers that you are sure to be in authority, or given authority, throughout life. These numbers are efficient and well-organized, so, taken together, they give you an extra shot of capability and a will that is difficult to appease. You ask a lot of yourself, but you are also very demanding of others, and short of sympathy for those you see as uninspired or lacking in imagination. This can be a problem for you, because the pressure you put on yourself to attain certain high standards in life – and, especially, critical praise for what you do – makes you easy prey for those who don't understand what you're trying to achieve. Jealousy of you will also be a problem at times, although usually your DAY/LIFE combination makes you fairly popular and well-recognized.

Relationships are a strange subject, because you value your freedom and the right to do things your own way. This means you may make things harder for yourself, and women with these two numbers often bypass any partner who could offer them financial security purely because they don't like to relinquish control of their own affairs. Men with these numbers, on the other hand, may only be excited by a partner who is just as independent and driven as they are – which sets the tone for future competitiveness.

Impatience becomes a greater problem, when **1** is added to your **DAY 8**. So often these two numbers mean that, even in childhood, there is a sense of unstoppable drive to get on with life and do things: there is no time like the present for you, in every way. Don't let this instinct deprive you of fun or relaxation; otherwise, in middle age you could experience premature burn-out, or a loss of any thrill about life. Always remember that this pair of numbers belongs to someone with vision and ambition, and that working towards a cause will usually satisfy your feelings of self-worth.

Day with 2 Life

7 and **2** may be the numbers of talent, thinking and perfection, but they lack the killer instinct to get on with some things that need doing. This, you have! **8** coupled with LIFE **2** gives you a crucial awareness of living in the material world and, while you are genuinely generous and make life as comfortable for those near you as you can, you do have a sense of self (far more so than a **7** and **2**) that pushes you to get on in this world and be a voice to be heard. **8** gives you that forcefulness and drive, and even creates some tension with the **2** because it recognizes that being selfless and undemanding can be difficult for everyone. The **8** DAY number makes the often timid **2** ask for what you want, and makes you a highly effective spokesperson in all courts – and **2**'s intuition is a bonus. Your excellent instincts are now backed up by great judgement and the will to make things happen.

These numbers bestow serious musical ability and an appreciation for the rhythms of life, so that the talents of **2** may add dimension and gain efficiency through **8** every day. Equally, you may have an excellent sense of smell or a refined palate. **2** and **8** together generally improve one of the senses besides hearing, so you may be working very strongly through your physical awarenesses.

Hard work will not frighten you, and **2** with **8** makes it likely you'll push to work for yourself, or, especially, in a partnership, since **2** rules such things. Many will give up trying to keep up with you, but you know where you want to go, and you want to have fun getting there. You may – with that sense of rhythm – also be very good at sport, and physical release in sport, or with outdoor activity, is necessary to balance the energies you use to push yourself mentally and emotionally. **2** is very sensitive, and offsets **8**'s hardiness.

Relationships are important to you, and you want to be in love with someone who is a little bit special, out of the ordinary. This may not be someone whom everyone agrees is beautiful, but it will be someone you know is striking, and other opinions don't matter. Your destiny is to be in the world talking about something you are passionate about, and this you will do successfully. Your partner has to accept that they will be sharing you – and this is all the more true if your **2 LIFE** number happens to be master number **11**. Life will be full, that's for sure!

8 Day with 3 Life

This combination of numbers could be anything from a hurricane to a gentle breeze, for both numbers have power and people skills. Whether they huff and puff and blow your house down, or simply act as a breath of fresh air, will depend largely on circumstances.

Charming in social situations, you could blag the Crown jewels from a beefeater and still have time for tea – and my, don't you like to take tea in swish places! Your membership to the latest hip club is a requisite starting point, and when you join the school picnic you'll want to pack a hamper from an exclusive store, and spread out a cashmere tartan rug. **3** adds a little recklessness to **8**'s love of luxury. You'll also beat all the other parents in the family race just so you can say, 'I'm a terrible runner,' and woe betide someone who does not produce a formal

| 8 | 9 | 1 | 2 | 3 | 4 | 5 | 6 | 7 |

apology for missing your birthday!

For here is a blending of appreciation for quality and a generous nature. You are loved by all who work with you, and are known as the life and soul of the party. Most competitive with yourself, you expect others to give their all on every occasion, and anything less than perfect is not to be accepted. Vivacious and enticing, you can also be bad-tempered and moody, and your partner will have to be a very patient person. **3** demands colour from life and **8** is a power number, with the consequent effect that even fun is a serious business. True, you have an innate sense of what will fire the imagination of the marketplace, and if you don't work in television or PR your skills are wasted. Throwing yourself into each venture, be it American quilting or redecorating a whole room to complement one piece of furniture, your aesthetic eye has extra vision.

Just remember that your personal drive and need for results can be a burden to others, as not everyone moves at your pace or dances to your tune. But, if anyone needs a counsellor, or an ear, or a voice of quiet reason, yours is the one. You make light of what is heavy, and see a calm path across volcanic ground. The ease and charm with which you seemingly undertake each task is the envy of all around you, but be aware that not everyone has read the works of Shakespeare twice. Your passion for literature gives you a enquiring mind, but can make you a tad snobby about those less well-educated than you. The two sides of the **8**'s character are accentuated by the juggling **3**, making you good at many things but difficult to please.

Day with 4 Life

'Mogul' or 'tycoon' are words that spring to mind when one considers the number **4** married to the superior business skills that come with your **DAY 8**. This may sound overly materialistic, but fortunately there is some creative flow as well.

While these two numbers pull against each other when seated in two individual personalities, operating within one person they lend each other utterly desirable attributes. **8** becomes more earthy, less philosophical and more in touch with other people's everyday problems, while **4** gains from **8**'s excellent judgement, impartiality, and ability to see both sides of every story. As a result, **4**'s moodiness is less pronounced, and the high-minded **8** leads worthy **4** to be more broad-minded and less serious. **8** also raises **4**'s reason-conscious mind to more spiritual

7   6   5   4   3   2   1   9   8

questions, and often allows **4** to find some form of religious or spiritual expression – although it will always be grounded in what seems reasonable.

With its feet firmly planted on the ground, **4** is often nimble at sporty activities, but **8** adds rhythm and turns **4** into a truly gifted athlete. Similarly, **8**'s musicality governs **4**'s skill with their hands, and frequently makes a hard-working but talented soloist of you; you should at least have some ability in one of these directions. In fact, either of these fields may become your chosen vocational path. And then there's **8**'s insatiable desire for a fine library: this takes **4**'s literary interests to a new level and adds excellent critical judgement. Overall, if LIFE **4** makes **8** enviably practical, DAY **8** lifts **4**'s gaze to a higher pinnacle. Each number improves the other's shortcomings – especially in relationship terms. **8** is a more exciting partner, but, added to **4**'s reliability, offers the loved one a lasting and growing relationship full of surprises. Love becomes more solid.

8	9	1	2	3	4	5	6	7

The most interesting manifestation of an **8/4** combination is the capacity to achieve — all by yourself — the high-quality material goods that you may wish for. Add to this the fact that generous **8** loosens **4**'s zealous guard of the purse strings, and you are bound to spoil those nearest and dearest to you in the nicest restaurants or the most luxurious holiday resorts. **8** also ensures the managerial status which your LIFE number **4** deserves.

8 Day with 5 Life

Wow! **5** and **8** make a beautiful pairing. **5** is sociable and entertaining, with an eye for the slightly eccentric things in life, while **8** is socially skilled par excellence. The combination of these two numbers makes you an unquestionable success in business. With two such similar numbers, the parts of **5** and **8** which complement each other mean you're a fascinating and exciting person to be around. **5**'s love of partying combined with **8**'s effortless command of any situation means that – for you – the after-office hours are as much about thrilling business matters as those spent in the boardroom. **8**'s subtle awareness of others' feelings allows **5**'s flair for mixing any set of people together to shine even more – making you the host or hostess of the year on many occasions.

5 has an eye for colour, design and the arts, but **8**

| 8 | 9 | 1 | 2 | 3 | 4 | 5 | 6 | 7 |

channels this creativity into more tangible properties with more intellectual applications – often writing, or television. Whenever your **5** side is feeling laid-back or uninspired, **8** can rescue you, and help you to carry on till late to finish a piece of work, or take on extra work when necessary. **8** has a propensity to worry about things that the **5** would consider out of your hands, and there are occasionally a devil and an angel on your shoulder, arguing pragmatism against spontaneity. Sometimes **8** can be too hard on itself, though, and **5** helps to remind you of the good things in your life, just kicking back and relaxing being exactly what **5** does best.

8/5 makes an affectionate pair of numbers, though you may be equally bold – and sometimes intimidating – about love. **5** is a sexual feline waiting to pounce, while **8** seems frighteningly together ... so much so, that potential partners are sometimes scared off by the thought of such a precocious and unnerving lover. **5**s value their independence and this sometimes makes relationships difficult, yet **8** wants to be loved by an equal. You are torn between the attraction to partners who are driven and independent like yourself, and to those who need you around.

With **5**'s impatience and **8**'s high mind, you have no time for those who aren't keeping up with you. **5** always moves ahead quickly, frustrating those around them, and this is exacerbated by your **DAY 8**'s need to keep progressing at all times. Fools are not tolerated by either of these numbers. **8**'s drive to get on with life can sometimes blind **5**'s need for fun – but don't let it. Others love the charming, sociable person you are, and there is nothing in this world that could make you take your eye seriously off the ball for long – even if it tried.

Day with 6 Life

This is an extremely lucky combination of numbers, as **8** can sometimes be a bit of a dragon to contend with, but **6** gives you the gentle personableness necessary to put your fire-breathing techniques to best use. While **6** often prefers to contribute to other people's creative skills, **8**s have more meteoric aspirations of their own, not content to watch others do a job they know they could do better. They will always jump head first into a project that they are convinced will be a success – and, with a **DAY 8/LIFE 6** pairing, you are usually right. **6**'s ineffable charm and peacemaking skills give **8**'s power of eloquence and entrepreneurial talent the scope to soar – and the sky doesn't even begin to be your limit. You could take control of your world like a baby tycoon dominating a Monopoly board – cool and unnoticed until you've cleaned up!

6's skills in so many areas can sometimes be a burden, but **8** channels the creativity into exciting and enticing new projects. **6** will have met and charmed the next big thing in the art world in a small café in Soho, but **8** makes certain they are signed to your publishing company before the lattes have even arrived. **8**s are charming and versatile all on their own, but that is intensified in this pairing. **6**'s easy-going attitude, which puts everyone at ease, is combined with **8**'s electric appeal and occasional necessary ruthlessness to make a captivating person everyone is in awe of.

Despite **8**'s unquestionable charm and visible 'outsider' appeal, they can often be very deep and private people, and are certainly stubborn and unrelenting characters once 'in the groove'. In an **8/6** pairing, **6**'s sometimes selfish stubbornness can be magnified to make you a little unbending at times, and you need to remember that not everyone sees things as plainly as you do. **6** will never complain openly about the silly or cheap choice of gift someone has given them, or the inadequacy of the thanks received for a favour rendered, but **8** will make such complaints clearly heard through other discreet but punitive means. (The lesson here, if you know an **8/6**, is to be sure to pick a small tasteful present of good quality for their birthday!)

What is excellent, though, is that **6** reins in **8**'s impatient nature to make sure that, even though **8** has no time for fools, the necessary care is taken to gather information from odd sources. **6** and **8** are both personable, and you really are beloved by those who know you. You are friendly and sympathetic, and always have reservations at the best restaurants. But even affable **6** has moments when the fire-breathing **8** in you rears its head! Enjoy it – how often do we get to say exactly what we want?

8 Day with 7 Life

This is an intellectual and reflective pair of numbers. **8** can dominate other numbers with its sheer veracity and force of will, but **LIFE 7** smooths out its noble intentions, allowing **8** to blend in, with less directness and more tact. **8** is sensitive of others' feelings, and **7** is aware of what is below the surface: together these numbers give you X-ray vision and an uncanny sense of what is developing. **8** is also a very godly number – in a rather ecumenical sense – and **7**'s spirituality controlling this energy can lead to some astonishing realizations and understanding. Anyone with birthday numbers of **8** and **7** together will prompt friends and family to personal epiphanies at 'crossroads' moments.

The bad news is that your lack of tolerance for foolish minds and shallow thinkers just doubled! **8** only associates with inquisitive and disciplined minds, so add this to **7**'s dignity and you've got a problem coping with banality. However, even in a room full of humourless automatons, having these numbers inherent in your mind-set helps you float to the clouds and come back with some material advantage. And it is good for **7** – often a little unaware of the need to live in a material world – to have the more practical and financially minded **8** leading the way. **8** really does like to earn money – not least because it is hugely generous, and likes the freedom to roam mentally that money enables. **7** doesn't mean to be cautious about funds, but often doesn't have that freedom to act spontaneously because money has not been a priority.

On the skill front, **7** partnering **8** brings serious musical ability and interest – and also, perhaps, a love of, or aptitude for, sports. **8** has such talent and rhythm; **7** adds that concentrated awareness that hard work is required if a talent is to be more than just that. **8/7** needs a good and extended education to support the intellectual wanderings it wishes to make. And you will very much need to be loved, because **8** is a harmonic number, offering an orchestral prelude to **7**'s solo virtuosity.

Despite **8**'s unquestionable charm, it often lacks self-discipline, but **7** evens this out. **8**, once it has tasted success, has amazing powers of organization at home, and also outside in the wider world. **7**'s analytical strengths add well to **8**'s good judgement to produce a fine mind with an old soul, and someone who – although you like people – will never be truly at home with the common crowd. Though **7** is not always adaptable, **8**'s talents paving the way give you authority and recognition, allowing you perhaps to find that judicious balance between the more public and the more private sides of your nature.

Day with 9 Life

A **DAY 8** with a **LIFE** number of **9** will be a wise old owl! Already humorous, **8** gets an extra pinch of wit from **9**, which assures not only that your peers pay you homage for your excellent mind and aura of knowledge, but also that they hang on your every word. The bon mot is a daily occurrence from you, and you will find yourself requited over and again. Perhaps the perfect life would see you writing the headlines for the newspaper you already own!

A **LIFE** number of **9** allows you to feel very deeply for other people, but you can sometimes be impressionable and take on too many of life's responsibilities. This is where **DAY 8** avoids calamity, for although **8** is always willing to be all things to everyone, its organizational expertise allows you to take control more dispassionately. A female **8**, for instance, howls with agony if a stocking ladders or a nail breaks, but if someone has a ruptured artery or falls down the stairs and breaks a leg, they can handle it without missing a beat. This is vital for **9**, always participating in the pain, and that raft of security that is deep within an **8**'s character helps you overcome the disappointments **9**s so often have thrust upon them. Your LIFE **9** is guilty of enticing you to give to other people to the point of personal detriment, but, oddly enough, **8** sees all and keeps things in check.

So, an **8/9** will have both a perceptive and a practical mind (thanks to **8**) and intelligent eloquence (thanks to **9**). These combined talents surely see you shimmy your way up the pole of achievement. You may be attracted to performing arts or government work, because these two numbers together suddenly become very public and flirt with fame. Or, literature and other forms of writing – even dramatic, since **9** is so strongly concerned with drama and film – may be your overwhelming desire. In any field, **8** has the nous and **9** the raw talent to make any competitors feel like amateurs. Both numbers together also make you more sexy, sultry and secretive.

In short, **9** has the flair to sashay down the street with a warm and friendly outward manner that attracts comment and admiration from passers-by, while **8** helps you do this with heels on. Both numbers are travelling – up, out, away. Nothing stays stagnant, and no goal remains the only goal, when you dance to the beat of these two numbers. A great host or hostess, with a busy, delving mind, you will make others breathless watching what you get though in a month. That would be another's lifetime!

THE FUTURE
Take a look what's in store...

And now we come to the calculation of your future.
Each year, on your birthday, you move into a new
sphere of number-influence which governs that year.
The numbers progress in cycles of nine years; after
nine years, the cycle starts over again, and a whole
new period of your life begins afresh. The cycle can
be applied to every number, so you can discover what
the main issues will be for partners, friends and
family, as well as for yourself, in any given year (*see
calculation instructions, opposite*). Emphasis is placed
on what will happen to you when you are in your
own year number – that is, in any '**8**' year cycle.

| 8 | 9 | 1 | 2 | 3 | 4 | 5 | 6 | 7 |

Working out your cycle

To find out what year you're currently in, use the same formula employed for calculating the LIFE number, but substitute the current year for the year in which you were born. Every year, the cycle then moves on by one more number until, after a **9** year, returning to **1**, to begin the cycle again.

Calculation example 1

BIRTHDAY: 17 March 1971

TO CALCULATE THE
CURRENT YEAR NUMBER: $1+7+3+\underbrace{[2+0+0+7]}_{\text{CURRENT YEAR}} = 20$, and $2+0 = $ **2**

*This means that on 17 March 2007 you move into a **2** year. On 17 March the following year, this would then move into a **3** year (1+7+3+2+0+0+8 = 21, and 2+1 = **3**), and the year after that, a **4** year, and so on.*

| 7 | 6 | 5 | 4 | 3 | 2 | 1 | 9 | 8 |

Calculation example 2

BIRTHDAY: 26 September 1962

TO CALCULATE THE   2+6+9+$\underbrace{2+0+0+7}_{\text{CURRENT YEAR}}$ = 26, and 2+6 = **8**
CURRENT YEAR NUMBER:

*This means that on 26 September 2007 you move into an 8 year.
On 26 September the following year, this would then move into a
9 year (2+6+9+2+0+0+8 = 27, and 2+7 = 9), and the year after
that, a 1 year, and so on.*

Many numerologists feel that the impact of a year number
can be felt from the first day of that year – in other words,
from 1st January. However, the usual school of thought is
that the new number cycle is initiated *on your birthday
itself*, and my experience tends to corroborate this. So,
if your birthday is fairly late in the year – November or
December, say – this means that you will have gone
through most of the calendrical year before *your new*

| 8 | 9 | 1 | 2 | 3 | 4 | 5 | 6 | 7 |

number-year cycle for that year begins.

Look back over some recent years, and see if – in the descriptions on the following pages – you can pinpoint the moment when your yearly number-cycle for any given year became apparent. You'll be amazed at just how accurate this system seems to be.

7   6   5   4   3   2   1   9   8

A 1 year

This is the perfect time to set up new and quite specific long-term goals, and consider just where you want to be a few years from now. You will have new people around you from this point on, and fresh ideas about them and the interests they awaken in you. This is a completely new chapter in your life, and you should set goals for a better and more fulfilling future.

Career-wise, a **1** year often occurs at a time of new employment, or of a complete change in direction in your working life. You are probably wanting to develop new skills or make use of untested talents. You have to believe in yourself now. This is the time when it's a little easier to step back and see how to get started along a particular path. Goals, you will understand, are perfectly attainable, even if a year ago they seemed unrealistic. In a **1** year you have tremendous focus and independence, and excellent determination.

The secret to your success now is in your ability to concentrate; but, emotionally, things can be quite testing. No matter how strong a love bond may be in your life, a **1** year demands that you do much for yourself. You could feel isolated or unsupported, even if someone dear is close by. This is a test of your own courage and inner strength. Only your strongest desires will gain results ... but then, your desires should be fierce during this cycle. Try not to act impulsively, as the push to do so will be powerful, but also, don't be afraid to be independent and go your own way. Strong urges are driving you – forward, for the most part – and a **1** year lends you exceptional clarity and energy.

A 2 year

A year which demands co-operation and partnerships at every level, **2** is a gentle year cycle, when you can consolidate what you started in the previous twelve months. You will need to be diplomatic and sensitive towards other people's feelings, but your intuition is very strong now, and you are able to share the load and the initiative more than you were allowed last year. For this reason, don't try to push things too far or too fast. After the previous whirlwind year, this is a moment to take your time and get things right.

Relationships come more into focus during a **2** year. This is especially pleasing if someone new entered your life in the last year or so, for the vibration of **2** helps a bond to strengthen, and a feeling of mutuality improves now. In some ways you may feel the desire or the need to be secretive, but this is because there are unknown elements at work all on fronts. It will affect you at work and at play, and in a close tie you will discover new tenderness that will probably separate you from other friends. If there is no one special currently in your life, this may be the year to find someone: a **2** year brings a relationship much stronger than a fling!

Your negotiation skills and ability to guess what another person is feeling may work very well for you this year; and, if the number **2** derives from master number **11** (which it almost surely will), there is a chance for serious partnerships and master opportunities. You will need to look at contracts carefully, and spend time on legalities. But this is often the most exciting and unusual year out of the nine. Mysteries come to light, and your ideas flow well. Just be prepared to consider another person in every equation.

A 3 year

Time for you! This twelve-month period is concerned with developing your abilities and testing your flexibility. Your imagination is especially strong, and you may have particular opportunities to improve your wealth and make lasting friendships. You will also need to be focused, because the energy of a **3** year is fast and furious, and may make you feel dissolute. Usually, though, this is a happy year spent with some travel prospects and many creative inspirations. Difficulties which intruded in the previous two years are often resolved in this year cycle.

Business and your social life often run together in a **3** year, and work will be a lot of fun. It is worth taking time over your appearance and indulging yourself more than usual, for the sociability of this number brings you many invitations and a chance to create a new look, or to explore

8   9   1   2   3   4   5   6   7

other aspects of your personality. You have extra charm this year, so try to use it where it is needed.

Many people find that the number **3** expresses itself in a year cycle as a third person to consider: frequently, this is the birth of a child or an addition to the family, but it might be that another party pressures you in your personal relationship. Don't talk too much about this, or show nervousness. Under a **3** vibration, it is easy to become exhausted – even through over-excitement – so be alert to the impulse towards extravagance and fragmentation. Try to enjoy the way in which you are being drawn out of yourself this year, and allow yourself time to study, write, paint. Anything you really want you can achieve now – even strange wishes and desires can be pulled towards you. Make sure you think a little about what you are asking for!

A 4 year

A much-needed year of good-housekeeping – on the personal level, as well as literally. This year will demand practicality from you. Often a **4** brings a focus on money or accounts, on repairs around the home, or on putting your life into better order. It may not be what you want, yet it will force itself upon you. It is sometimes a year spent with a pen in hand – writing lists or cheques, doing sums and keeping diaries. It is also a year when you will need to do some research, to find out about what you don't know.

You have so much work to do in a **4**, or **22**, year – more than for a long time. Your personal pleasure takes second place to requirement, and it may seem difficult to stick to the task sometimes. Money demands that you do so, for extra expenditure is not advised in this twelve-month period. Yet if this sounds stressful, it also gives you a feeling of satisfaction that you will achieve so much this year – a job of hard work and dedication really well done. It may be that this year gives you a very good foundation for the future and sets up lasting improvements.

You will never survive a **4** – or, especially, a **22** – year if you are not organized and implement a system of work and life. Be honest in what you do with others, but also in what you do for yourself. You cannot deceive yourself, and must check details carefully. You may have a feeling of burden at times, but there is a chance to feel you have done something extraordinary, too. Translate your clever ideas into practical results. The most significant thing for you to do is to concentrate on proper personal management. The weight of the world is on your shoulders, but you can bear it if the preparations you make are good. There is no escape from demands on your time and intelligence, but nothing can be hurried, so face the job ahead and you will soon find you have climbed a hill to new vistas.

7   6   5   4   3   2   1   9   8

A 5 year

After careful management of your time last year, and a feeling of being tied to the wheel, this will seem like bursting from the inside of a darkened room into bright light. Now you have a change from routine to madness, and you may feel a personal freedom that was denied you last year. Nevertheless, nothing is completely settled in a **5** year, and this uncertainty may take its toll. Try to look at this cycle as a chance to find success in newer areas, and a way to advance from necessary stagnation into running waters of energy and vitality. You will update your sense of yourself during this period, and make progress towards the life you want, following the previous year's required self-discipline.

You are admitting to the need for new pastures, so your ideas of what your life might include, or who may have a role in it, may alter now. No one likes to be held back in

8   9   1   2   3   4   5   6   7

a **5** year, but it is still important not to be too hasty in your actions. Use your energies, by all means, but govern them with your head. This is the time for innovation, and new takes on old goals, but if you quarrel with those dear to you, or with whom you work, it may be difficult to repair later. If change is still inevitable, be as kind and constructive as possible, and make sure you aren't leaping from one difficult situation straight into another. You need to discover your versatility and personal resourcefulness to get the best out of this cycle. And, for some of the twelve months, travel or lots of movement seems inescapable.

This year is potentially some kind of turning point for you. Learning how to adapt to sudden circumstances is vital, because any plans or directives set in stone will cause you pain, and possibly come unstuck. Be prepared for changes and, if this brings a nervousness with it, try to meet the adventure head-on. If you talk yourself up and take on a front-running position, you can work wonders in a **5** year.

A 6 year

Love is in the air. Other things seize your time too – your home needs attention, and duties demand your energy – but, principally, this year is about emotions and relationships. Sometimes love and happiness are a reward for surviving so much in the past two years, and for unselfish service and support for others. The emphasis is on finding harmony with others, and this may come in various ways. This year, you may have the impetus and opportunity to erase problems that have previously beset you. You understand, and feel acutely sensitive towards, others, and are more radiant and beautiful than you have been for some time. If you can be kind and positive in emotional dealings, you will benefit in many ways, including materially.

There are hurdles in a **6** year in connection with obligations you feel towards others. At times you are stretched,

| 8 | 9 | 1 | 2 | 3 | 4 | 5 | 6 | 7 |

because there are personal desires and ties you want to nurture which are countermanded by the duties you are subjected to. You may resent this, yet, if you can remain cheerful, you will be rewarded in ways not immediately apparent. Love is trying to sweep you off your feet, but your health may suffer because you are trying to fit in so much, and the intensity of your feelings is strong.

While it's good to be helpful in a **6** year, don't allow yourself to be taken advantage of, or let people drain you completely. Set up a system that lets you delegate some responsibility. Your home may bloom while you're in such a happy mood, and you should feel creative and mellow. The events of a **6** year are not as fast and furious as the previous year, but things move steadily towards a happier state of being. Let the time go as it will, because this is not a year to fight against what comes to you; get into the right philosophical gear and open yourself to pleasant surprises that come from being useful, and being warm with others.

A 7 year

This year is a time for manifesting your goals by visualizing them. See yourself triumphing and continuing toward your vision. Never lose sight of what you want, or confusion will reign. You'll be tempted this way and that, annoyed by gossip, and attacked by those who love you but don't understand what you are trying to do. Don't be swayed by them, or you will lose your opportunities and precious time.

Keep your head, as everything depends on your state of mind. Refuse to react to distractions, and avoid hasty actions or sudden decisions. A calm approach is the best remedy to the chaos surrounding you. You may have to move house without warning, but take it in your stride and make a calm, clear choice on where to go. If you are travelling somewhere exotic, be prepared with vitamins and medicines to avoid viruses of any kind.

Legal matters may arise during this year, relating to business, investments or house options. Consult an expert to avoid pitfalls, and, when you feel happy, proceed with confidence. If you have taken all the facts and details into account, you'll now be within sight of your goal. But watch your health, as the number 7 is connected with this subject for both good and ill. You might get fit and lose some weight or, conversely, suffer with some little grievance. This is a time for mental, spiritual and physical detoxing. Also, rest: take a vacation to the country, to a quiet location where you can think in peace. Let no one confuse you. You may have to wait, but you will know how to come out on top if you listen to your intuition.

This is an excellent year for study, research, writing and reading, and clearing out all the unnecessary people or ideas from your past.

7   6   5   4   3   2   1   9   8

An 8 year

Your own year cycle brings the possible finding of a soulmate. If you're single, you couldn't have a better chance of meeting that special someone than now. **8** years also relate to money, so you may be caught up with an impossible workload and regard the arrival of such a potentially strong love as poor timing – and perhaps this is why it comes to you, because your attention being taken up elsewhere may be the best reason for someone's admiration. The love vibration you experience under karmic year **8** may point to a future relationship prospect which has a lasting importance.

For those in settled relationships, pregnancy sometimes comes with this number, and it brings a very special link between the child and their parents. Or, you may experience a deep urge to study a subject that comes easily to you, though you have never learned about it before – a

8   9   1   2   3   4   5   6   7

language, perhaps, or an artistic skill you were attracted to but never developed, but which you now pick up well. Even a professional subject that you seem to grasp quickly will seem more important to perfect than ever before. Partly, this is because **8** year cycles concern making more money, and dealing with the deeply felt past. There are huge opportunities for you in an **8** year, and you will want to be prepared to maximize them. However, you'll need to use good judgement and be efficient with your time management.

Many people feel pushed to the limit in an **8** year, because there's just so much going on. But consider that the vibration of the number wants to find positive expression, so the more efficiency and determination you can bring to it, the better the chance of finishing on a high note. Don't over-commit your time or money, and be ready to acquiesce to others' ways of doing things. Be confident, but ready to adjust too. **8** is made up of two circles, asking 'infinity' of you. But this year, you can do it if anyone can!

A 9 year

Your personal affairs all come to a head in a **9** year, and whatever has been insufficient, or unsatisfying, will rise to the surface and demand change now. It could be the fulfilment of many dreams, for this is the culmination of nine years' experience. Whatever is jettisoned was probably no longer of use – though this might seem dispassionate. Many friendships will drift away, but you have probably outgrown them. The strongest demand of you is a readiness to discard what will not be part of your serious future – and this can mean a temporary feeling of insecurity.

You will certainly travel in a **9** year. Even if a trip is short, or of no great distance, it will settle something in your mind. The more compassionate, tolerant and forgiving you are, the more warmth and generosity will come to you. This is not the right moment to start something completely new, but if events arise as a natural conclusion to what has gone before, this is a good thing. Your mind needs to engage with bigger issues, for selfishness or petty ideas will cause you unhappiness under this number. People will thwart you in your career and personal matters — and these obstacles seem to come out of the blue, and are beyond your control. However, if you think on philosophical issues and remain open to big ideas, everything will turn out well.

A **9** year can be populated with many friends and activities, yet can feel lonely too; this is a cycle for completion of tasks and the ending of what is not enduring. But this is the right time to see the fruits of your previous work. Be wise about where your destiny seems to want to take you. Your artistic and imaginative facilities are inspired now, and you'll begin to see new directions that you know you must investigate in the years ahead. You know what is missing in your life, or where you've failed yourself, and can now prepare for the new adventure that's about to dawn.

7   6   5   4   3   2   1   9   8

How to find your DAY NUMBER

Add the digits for the day of birth, and keep adding them until they reduce to one number:

EXAMPLES

17 March 1971   1+7 = **8**

26 September 1962   2+6 = **8**

How to find your LIFE NUMBER

Add the digits for the day, month and year of birth, and keep adding them until they reduce to one number:

EXAMPLES

17 March 1971   1+7+3+1+9+7+1 = 29
                       2+9 = 11 (a 'master' number), and 1+1 = **2**

26 September 1962   2+6+9+1+9+6+2 = 35
                       and 3+5 = **8**

Further reading

The Complete Book of Numerology, David A. Phillips, Hay House, 2006

The Day You Were Born: A Journey to Wholeness Through Astrology and Numerology, Linda Joyce, Citadel Press, 2003

Many Things on Numerology, Juno Jordan, De Vorss Books, 1981

Numerology, Hans Decoz and Tom Monte, Perigee Books, 2001

Numerology: The Romance in Your Name, Juno Jordan, De Vorss Books, 1977

Sacred Number, Miranda Lundy, Wooden Books, 2006

The Secret Science of Numerology: The Hidden Meaning of Numbers and Letters, Shirley Blackwell Lawrence, New Page Books, 2001

About the author

Titania Hardie is Britain's favourite 'Good Witch' and a best-selling author. Born in Sydney, Australia, Titania has a degree in English and Psychology, and also trained in parapsychology and horary astrology. With a high media profile, she regularly appears on television in the UK, US, Canada, Australia and South Africa, as well as receiving widespread newspaper and magazine coverage. Her previous titles have sold over a million copies worldwide, and include *Titania's Crystal Ball*, *Aroma Magic*, and *Hocus Pocus*. Her first novel is due to be published in summer 2007.

Acknowledgements

Many thanks to you, Nick, for the clear and brilliant vision; you knew what you wanted and, like a true and inspired **1**, kept mulling it over until a way was found. This is your baby. Also big thanks to Tessa, master number **22**, for your commitment to this magnum opus beyond call: only you and I know, Tessa, how much time and soul has gone into all of these words. To Ian, for keeping us piping along with a true **4**'s sanguine approach to such a long body of work, and to Elaine and Malcolm for the look – **6**s, naturally! For my daughter Samantha, thanks for some of your ideas which found expression in the second-to-last section: I love the latte in Soho while signing the author. Let's see! To Georgia, for work in the field on number **5**, my thanks. To all of you, my appreciation, and I wish you all LUCKY NUMBERS!

EDDISON·SADD EDITIONS

Editorial Director Ian Jackson
Managing Editor Tessa Monina
Proofreader Nikky Twyman

Art Director Elaine Partington
Mac Designer Karen Watts
Production Sarah Rooney